Creative

Crafts

for

Everyone

Creative

Crafts

G. ALAN TURNER

for

A STUDIO BOOK

Everyone

THE VIKING PRESS · NEW YORK · 1959

To Julie, Jill, and Steven,

and all those who enjoy imaginative challenge

Contents

What This Book Is About

THIS IS A BOOK of ideas for imaginative people who like to create things.

Those who can say "I made it myself" are the fortunate ones, the creative people we all admire. Our book is for them—and for the surprising number of others who haven't yet realized how simple it is to join their ranks.

Everything in this book is a challenge to your ingenuity, and most of the ideas take advantage of low-cost or no-cost materials. Here are projects that are actually adventures in good taste. And best of all, they have *practical use*. Holiday ornaments and decorations; home-furnishing ideas, fabric designs, and tableware; distinctive clothing and smart accessories—hundreds of ideas to add sparkle to your home, classroom activities, and personalized gift-giving.

There is no limit to what you can do by exercising the artist's gift of imagination. And this book points the way.

Cardboard egg cartons are easily decorated with tempera colors. For permanency, such as when using them as candy dishes for children's parties, coat entire surface with clear shellac.

[10]

1

Papercraft

Paper magic! Gay holiday wrappings, tree ornaments, party favors, unusual greeting and place cards, toys. All are made with the most inexpensive of art materials:bright papers, cardboard, paste and glitter, a pair of scissors, and some brilliant tempera colors. Additional decorating can be done with crepe papers, cotton, and spun glass. All coloring of paper should be done with tempera colors (poster paint), but, if you work on metallic papers, switch to Dek-All, which adheres to smooth surfaces without crawling.

Tempera on Paper

Tempera paints are a popular medium for young artists and hobbyists because they dry quickly, are applied simply, and cost little. Temperas also wash off hands and clothing without staining. They are available in premixed jars or as a dry powder to which water is added. The latter type is suggested for larger projects and for schoolroom use. It stores well and, being dry, does not lose water to form a hard cake. (Dried-out tempera may be restored by simply adding more water, allowing it to stand over-night, and then thoroughly mixing it with a stick.) A pint of tempera powder will make two quarts of liquid. This same tempera powder also makes excellent finger paint, by the way. (Just add some liquid laundry starch to it.) Another well-known use for tempera is in painting large areas of backgrounds and scenery for amateur plays and displays.

Some uses of tempera colors for decorating paper products follow.

As water color

Add water to tempera powder, mixing slowly with a stick until desired consistency is reached. Obviously, the more water added, the more transparent the color. Tempera will adhere to many other surfaces in addititon to paper; use it on glass, cardboard, or even metal.

For stenciling

Do you want to do some simple stencil designs? Pounce your tempera mixture lightly with a cloth or wad of cotton through the open areas of the cutout stencil. You may also use a large brush, or spray on the mixture by thinning it somewhat and putting it in an insect spray gun, but pouncing is easier, being simply patting paint through the open areas.

For block printing

An inexpensive ink is prepared by adding one part varnish to three parts tempera powder. Mix this on a glass palette with a knife. The resulting ink is tacky and can be rolled with a rubber brayer onto the surface of your printing block.

Using Metallic Papers

Metal papers are stocked by all good art stores and are also available in rolls at department stores, where they are packaged as gift wraps. For most decorative effects you will probably find the solid hues and tints the most practical, rather than those with patterns already imprinted. Among the most popular colors available are gold, silver, red, copper, deep and light blue, greens, purple, and soft pastels. The stock is metalized on only one side, so in cutting decorative forms place two pieces of metal paper back to back. The two pieces are then pasted together, metal side out. You can draw your sketch directly on the uncoated side and use this as a cutting guide.

Cutouts should be simple and not so large that the weight of the paper causes them to buckle. Use them on Christmas trees as stars, snowflakes, and geometric shapes; use them for stylized greeting cards (by folding a piece in half, scissoring out your design, and then printing your message on the white stock inside).

Because the metallic surface is glossy, do your decorating with Dek-All. A thin coating of glue or shellac may be brushed across the mat side of the cutout to make it hard. You can then sprinkle on metal powders or glitter if you wish, while the glue or shellac is still wet.

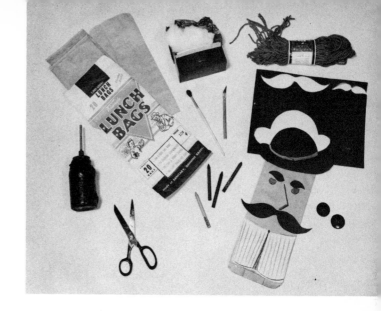

Basic materials for making paper-bag puppets include: cotton, wax crayons, buttons, knitting yarn, construction paper, tempera colors, glue, and, of course, the versatile paper bag. *(Photo: Daniel Firestone)*

Paper-bag Puppets

Paper bags—twenty hand puppets for a dime! Digging into the kitchen bric-a-brac drawer, some second-graders came up with the following loot: odd-sized buttons, knitting yarn, scissors and paste, some crayon stubs, and a wad of cotton. With a few deft touches, these homely oddments were transformed into the decorative features for a wild assortment of sack puppets.

What'll you have? A Gay Nineties dandy? Hobo? Clown? Just cut, draw, and paste. Yarn becomes hair and can be affixed with library paste, rubber cement, or a stapler. The hand puppets become delightful companions for shut-ins or youngsters who get underfoot on a rainy afternoon. They are slipped over the hand and, when necessary, can be secured with a rubber band.

Other thoughts for decorating: eyes made of bottle caps, cutout construction paper, gumdrops; mouth from penny "watermelon" candies; teeth from seeds or dried corn kernels; nose that was formerly a cotton ball, cough drop, gumdrop, or marshmallow.

Clothing can be pasted-on fabric scraps; paper place settings or doilies make excellent collars and dickies. Leftover striped Christmas wrapping paper is fine for a clown's shirt.

When you are cutting out construction paper, the entire puppet face or the individual parts can be lightly drawn with a soft pencil, then the paper can be scissored from these areas and transferred to the bag. (The cutout holes make good stencils, by the way, if direct application of crayon or chalk is desired.) There is lots of fun with these modernized applications of a traditional idea.

[13]

Anyone can make these simple paper-bag puppets—in fifteen minutes or less. Large bags with similar decoration and with holes made for eyes and nose can be used as Halloween masks. *(Photo: Daniel Firestone)*

Opposite page, top: Paper-bag puppets decorated with lollipops, cotton tufts, gumdrops, yarn, buttons, and corn kernels. Additional details are applied with wax crayons or poster paints. *(Photo: Daniel Firestone)*

Opposite page, bottom: Three paper gentlemen made of crepe paper, gummed stars, drinking straws, and paper bags. Jaunty feather in hat is pipe cleaner, eyes of center mask are candy cups. *(Photo: Dennison Manufacturing Company)*

Paper Chains

Long pendent strips of metallic paper are cut into segments of four to six inches and these are laid flat for easy decorating with poster paint or Dek-All. Sketch on designs or personalize with first names of guests and family. The segments are then glued together in an interlocking chain and festooned across the room or hung as streamers from a tree.

Paper Birds and Insects

A galaxy of graceful forms made of paper, feathers, glitter, and string is illustrated in color opposite. Outline the forms on light white cardboard and cut out these basic shapes. Decorate with tempera. Bird tails can be made of cellophane or straws from a broom; feathers are from the plumage of an old hat. Each motif is cut out twice and the plumes or straws are sandwiched between them with glue. Heart shapes are pleated tissue paper, as are crinoline borders. Use oil colors for adding design motifs. Ends are closed with bits of gold or silver gift-wrap cord. On the Christmas-tree ornament, one end of cord can be used to hang ornament from tree or to tie it to a gift. Use tempera colors on tissue-paper sections.

Paper and Cardboard City

What youngster wouldn't be thrilled to make or get a magical city like the one printed in color opposite? Here's the procedure: Choose a motif that includes church, office building, homes, farmhouse and silo, or whatever your fancy dictates. For each building involved, sketch the outlines of four sides in a row, then leave an inch of blank for gluing the fourth and first sides together. Work directly on heavy cardboard stock or transfer your sketch with tracing paper. Next, paint in the details with tempera while the sketch is still flat on your drawing table. You may color in the windows or cut them out and tape pieces of colored cellophane or metallic paper across them from the back. (As a professional touch, you can even mount light bulb sockets on a table and then build the city with the bulbs inside each structure to simulate lighted windows. Be certain that a few ventilating holes are left and that the warm bulb does not come in contact with the cardboard.)

You are now ready to start building up the city. First, cut out the sections which will comprise the roof and walls and score the joining corners with a dull knife or scissors blade so they can be folded.

Glue the first and last sides together at a right angle with the one-inch paper overlap. Now, cut out your roof section, allowing it to hang over an inch or so for the eaves, then score it and fold it over the walls and tape securely in place. Additional wings to the building are made the same way, except that a fourth wall is eliminated. Round buildings (that is, roundhouse or silo) are constructed by making a tube of cardboard and stapling it. The floor is made of cardboard. Round roofs are made by cutting out a compass-drawn circle of construction paper and snipping away a pie-shaped wedge to close up for a slight cone shape. Scotch-tape or glue the round roof shut. City walls are scored lengths of cardboard.

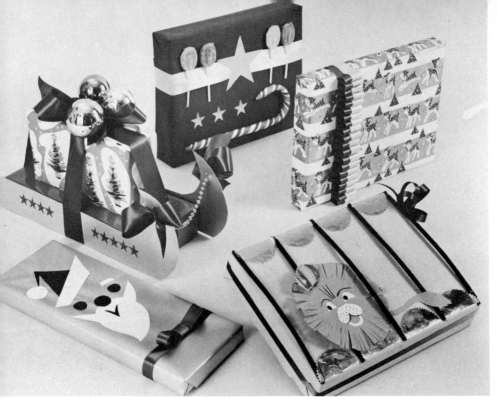

(Photo: Dennison Manufacturing Company)

Paper Gift Wraps

Wrapping a holiday gift is a science that goes far beyond sheathing it in bright paper and ribbon. An imaginatively designed package can turn the most inexpensive offering into something really special.

Five such gift wraps are shown here, reproduced to delight your eye and inspire you to seek new directions in this handicraft. Here's how the quintet of wraps are made:

Sleigh. This is for Mother or a special young lady. Topside is a bottle of perfume done up in gay little Christmas trees. Next is a large box wrapped in bright red. These gifts sit snugly in your cardboard sleigh, which has silver-colored gummed paper pasted on its runners and is further decorated with gummed stars. Tie the gifts aboard with green ribbon and some tiny gold and silver tree ornaments.

Lollipop Delight. A hypnotic sight for young eyes. Twice as much fun, for the wrap can be eaten too. Just make a simple wrap with metallic paper, make slits in the package ribbon, and tuck in a row of lollipops. Scatter on some gummed stars and, for a final touch, on goes a candy cane.

Fawns for Small Fry. Clever integration of a preprinted motif which appears on gift paper, with twisted red and white tyings to look like ribbon candy. The accordion loops are fastened with Scotch tape.

Languid Leo. Lion-hearted motif is meant for some rugged male. Design is simplified caricature cut from gummed paper of some bright color. First, cut out a circle, then fringe it with scissors to simulate mane of lion. Tail is also cut from same paper stock and pasted onto package. The cage is formed with black pipe cleaners (could be dipped in ink) and gold legal seals. Seals come as box of gummed labels.

Santa. This will please a young sophisticate. Cut the features out of colored paper and paste onto metallic wrapping paper. A red or green ribbon will finish it up.

Holiday gift wraps, hand decorated with stencils. Cut separate stencil for each color. When possible plan so motif is appropriate to the gift wrapped inside. *(Courtesy American Crayon Company)*

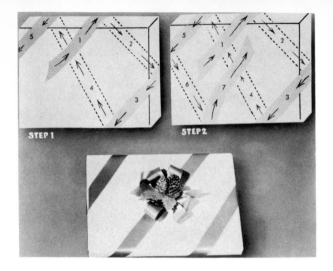

Candy-stripe ribbon tie looks especially pretty on solid-colored or small-patterned papers. Dotted lines represent position of ribbon on under side of box. Ribbon ends tie in center. (*Courtesy Dennison Manufacturing Company*)

How to tie it up

Now for some tips on wrapping procedure, as used by experienced personnel in large stores.

Always hold the starting end of a ribbon on the box with your left thumb. Use your right hand to bring the ribbon around the box. Go lengthwise first, then twist the leading part of the ribbon underneath the completed loop and circle the box in its shorter circumference. When you have thus circled the box in both directions, cut the ribbon and tie a knot. Make the bow separately, then tie it on with the two slight ends of the ribbon already on the box.

Gift wraps with harmonizing ribbons. Snowman, cut out of a thin white board, wears a hat and scarf of crepe paper. The white flower under tinsel ribbon is edged with silver glitter sprinkled over dabs of rubber cement.

Long, thin parcels can be tied by simply wrapping the ribbon two or three times about its short side. Do not try to make it all in one length; this usually looks messy. Instead, make each complete loop singly and either affix with tape or tie into a single knot, allowing two inches of ribbon to protrude from each end of knot as a simple bow.

Diagonal ribbons are applied by holding end with left thumb in one corner, going over corner and around to underneath side, then following to diagonally opposite corner. This is repeated until all four corners are circumscribed (see diagram). This can be a two-corner tie or a four-corner tie; just stop when you've achieved the desired effect. The secret is to keep the ribbon taut all the time with your left thumb, until the knot is securely tied.

Gay Christmas wraps combine printed papers with freehand decoration. Raised lettering spells "Noel" with cut ribbon glued into script shapes. Santa is a covered cereal box. Curls on his beard are made by pulling each cut strip of paper between the sharp edge of a scissor blade and a thumb pressed firmly against it.

MAKING CURLED RIBBON

Using a pair of scissors or dull kitchen knife, pull ribbed ribbon tautly along blade until it curls.

SOME DECORATING DEPARTURES

Let's take a few moments away from the conventional to discuss offbeat motifs which can add pertinency and distinction to your gift wraps. Keying your materials to the hidden contents of the box gives a provocative hint of its contents. For example, let's say you've chosen to give a fishing rod to someone. What are the qualities of such a gift? It is masculine, it is for a sporting enthusiast. Dainty gift wraps would be out of character. Some possibilities: select a sturdy wrap and tie it with a length of nylon rope (the kind found in government surplus stores, originally used for parachute shroud lines). Add color with a few stylized sketches of fishing lures, done in crayon or tempera. Complete the package by tying on a lure in a transparent plastic box.

Is it a bottle of precious perfume? A feminine wrap in subtle purple, dark blue, or silver might be appropriate. To leave little doubt, sprinkle on a few drops of perfume before wrapping away the gift. Your outer gift might then be a cut-glass perfume flask or atomizer, fastened with metallic cord and a pompon. (Or, why not a nosegay of lovely flowers?) By this method you have created a complete gift package with a preview teaser.

For a youngster's gift, you might design a pop-up Santa which is glued to the center of the package. It is constructed by folding metallic paper into an accordion (the neck); then gluing on a ping-pong ball as the Santa's face; dabbing on some eyes, a mouth, and a nose with nail polish or oil paint; and capping it all with a cotton beard. On Santa's head is perched a stocking cap fashioned by rolling a cone of red paper and gluing on more cotton for a snowy ball on top.

A FEW FINAL GIFT-WRAP IDEAS

Fresh out of themes for the package design? How about two simple white paper mittens with gay designs on them—flowers, mistletoe, snowflakes? Your gift card is neatly held between the facing mitts. Suggested gift-wrap paper colors: metallic red, pale pastels, or black.

Want some icicles to stream across your gift-wrap? Make them of white crepe paper, scissored with long, jagged edges. A bit of snow? Whip up a mixture of household soap chips or dishwashing detergent and water. Beat until it mounds just like real snow, then spatter across gift paper while still moist. When it dries, it will adhere to the gift and look just like the real thing!

Now you have the idea. Gift wrapping can be imaginative, creative fun.

Using Cellophane.

There's a lot you can do with cellophane. It is the basis for a sparkling decor to gift wrappings and party favors. A few twists of the wrist, a sheet of cellophane, a bit of tape, a pipe cleaner or two, and a marshmallow— and out comes an attractive doll! There's plenty of room for creative activity here.

In the photos shown here are some angels that look sweet enough to eat. And they are too, for their heads are made of marshmallows! Make several for holiday favors. You start with this equipment: sheets of colored cellophane, lightweight cardboard, pipe cleaners, marshmallows, bright ribbons, crayons, and a spool of thin wire.

The angel's robe is begun by cutting a small hole in the center of a sheet of cellophane. This will become the dress and halo. Rolling a cone

Making a choir angel out of cellophane. Base is made of cardboard, rolled into a cone shape. The skirt is cellophane.

A painted marshmallow head is impaled on a pipe cleaner. Wires, bent to form arms, are attached, then the entire unit is inserted in top of cone.

Cookie stacks can be quickly wrapped in colored cellophane for small and glamorous gifts. Use a circle of cardboard for the base and plastic ribbon for handles and bows. *(Photos: DuPont Company)*

of cardboard, tape it fast and slip the cellophane over the neck so the hole slips down and the skirt is suspended. Scotch-tape it in place and pinch it into pleats. Now, wrap a marshmallow in cellophane and let the twisted upper portion serve as a bonnet or halo. Tape it securely. Then poke a pipe cleaner through the bottom of the marshmallow and slip the end down into the cone as a neck. Facial features are added on the cellophane with oil paints.

For arms, simply bend two pipe cleaners at right angles and affix to the neck with wire. Poke loose ends of the arms out of sight into the cone or curl them into a tight spiral. You can add sleeves with cones of paper, and can add sparkle to any paper surface by dabbing it lightly with glue and then sprinkling glitter on it. Additional petticoats of cellophane may be added by cutting each circle slightly smaller than the previous one and slipping them over the body cone. (Try using different colors too!)

The third illustration on page 25 shows other motifs done in cellophane, including an edible Santa, a gift wrap for some chinaware, and a tier of cookies. In each case, some item of foodstuff or tableware forms the body of the gift wrap. In the case of Santa, his plump tummy is a round jar of canapes, crackers, or candy surmounted by a big ball of cheese. (Gouda and Edam are two of the more familiar varieties.) Fasten the two together with Scotch tape—the jar is the body and the cheese becomes the head. Wrap both in a single large sheet of red cellophane and tie a string around the neck space to delineate each. Now apply Santa's beard with tufts of cotton glued in place. His stocking cap is a cone of red cellophane made from a 7-by-10-inch sheet. Bend the point down sideways and pin on a maraschino cherry for a tassle. A couple of marshmallows would make fine buttons too. Finally, make him a belt of cotton pasted on green cellophane, with a silver-sprinkled buckle cut from cardboard. A sprig of holly adds the final touch to this different gift.

The cooky stacks are wrapped in colored cellophane, the top is twisted and tied with string, then a pompon of colored cellophane straws is taped to one side. A ribbon handle completes the job.

Using Papier-Mâché

To crafts enthusiasts, papier-mâché suggests a deep well of modeling experiences which never seems to run dry.

Materials for papier-mâché are elementary: newspapers, empty cardboard egg crates, scraps of bunting, tinsel, string, liquid starch or library paste, and water. Add your own props to these to produce unusual effects. The art materials employed to decorate the paper pulp are tempera paints, dye colors, and just about any coloring medium that will adhere to paper surfaces. The fastening of the component parts is done with library paste, liquid starch, masking tape, or staples.

Liquid laundry starch, toothpicks, powder tempera (to mix with starch for final coat of paint), facial tissues, and newspaper were used to make this papier-mâché rabbit. Masking tape is used to hold paper in shape. Mixture of liquid starch and facial tissue hardens sufficiently when dry to keep ears standing up without additional braces. At right, the finished rabbit after starching and painting.

As an example of papier-mâché sculpture, try constructing an animal form like a horse or donkey, or perhaps a giraffe. The initial step is one of observation; how does a horse stand, walk, swing its head? What pose is most characteristic? Now, what is the basic shape of a horse? Notice that this animal comprises a slender body, long legs, and an arched neck. Fine. Now you are ready to go to work.

Tear strips of newsprint to lengths of fifteen inches or more, then soak them in a pan of water until they are saturated to limpness. While this is going on, shape an armature of wire to serve as the rough skeleton about which the form will be built. For small projects, chicken wire makes a good armature; for larger ones, heavier-gauge wire or coat hangers may prove the best thing. Twist this wire about until it resembles the animal's form. In some cases you can get by without even using wire. You might substitute an empty milk or egg carton for the body, first spreading a coating of library paste over the waxed container to bind the papier-mâché.

Now, the soaked strips of paper are removed from the pan of water, blotted to remove excess moisture, then dipped through library paste and wrapped about the armature, gradually building up the form. When one

strip has been completed, overlap the next slightly and dab on a bit of paste to secure it and form a continous effect. Keep this up, completing each unit roughly and then bringing the next one up to the same degree of completion. Now cover the figure generously with library paste to form a smooth skin.

Prod and squeeze the pasty paper into shape, much as you would model in clay with your fingers. Don't worry about fine details yet; that comes last of all and is usually done with a blunt stick, pencil, or any handy instrument you wish to employ.

Allow the paste to dry. The joints of paper stripping will be almost invisible. The form is now ready for decoration. Add your details with paint or crayon. Once the undercoating has dried, you can add additional colors or crayon work. For more permanence, you can shellac the figure. (Do this before you add any props, of course.) Finally, props can be pasted or stapled on—buttons or bottle caps for eyes, bits of tinsel and glitter, twine, fabric, or cellophane. In addition to these props, the papier-mâché enthusiast may find use for craft papers, paper doilies, crepe papers, colored construction sheets, beads, bits of costume jewelry, and corks.

In addition to the wire armatures suggested, you can also use cardboard rolls (found in boxes of aluminum foil, Saran Wrap, paper toweling), vegetables, modeling clay, and even inflated toy balloons.

The paper-stripping method used for our animal form is not the only way one can work with papier-mâché. It is also possible to soak a large wad of paper and squeeze it into pulp, which may then be used just like modeling clay. Add enough paste to this wadding to make it pliable. If it dries before you have finished with your construction, more water and paste can be added. The pulp can also be strengthened and extended by mixing in sawdust, sand, or salt. Cleansing tissues of the Kleenex type need not be soaked in water. Just mix with paste and use this for fine detail work.

Small, lightweight papier-mâché forms sometimes do not require a wire or cardboard armature to support the paper. Simple animal forms can be made by merely rolling newspaper into tight rolls (to serve for the body and appendages). These are stapled or glued securely together, then a head is made by shaping it about a light bulb, ping-pong ball, or tennis ball. About this improvised modeling armature, a cover of wet paper is placed to make later removal of the object easy. (This will keep it free of paste.) The paper is wound and pasted about this until the form is built up. When dry, the object is slit gently in two and the bulb or ball removed from inside its papier-mâché nest. The halves are then joined with more paper and paste and decorated.

It is important to mention here that papier-mâché is a process free of rigid rules of procedure. Although the steps just described are logical and popular, you can evolve your own methods.

Theatrical groups consider papier-mâché a boon. In addition to its low construction cost and light weight, it also stands up under reasonable punishment.

Theatrical property departments have developed their own method for making papier-mâché objects. They prefer the pulp procedure and prepare pulp in large quantities in the following manner:

Newspapers are shredded and boiled in water until they turn to pulp. The mash is then scooped out of the vat and dumped in a cloth sack (a burlap bag or laundry bag will do). The excess water is removed by squeezing. Large sacks are handled by walking over them. The pulp is then emptied into another container filled with sizing, to form modeling mash. Size is made by adding one quart liquid glue to two parts of water, or two cups of flour to a gallon of water. You can substitute equal amounts of library paste and water, if no flour is handy, but the mixture is rather flexible and you should experiment until you reach the preferred consistency.

If you want to remove all ink from the newspaper, bleach it with a solution of lye or scouring powder. If you wish to add color to the mash itself instead of later painting it, add powder tempera color to the sizing solution. You may also use clothing dyes and, in a pinch, drop in pieces of colored crepe paper, which will bleed and tone the mixture.

This soaked pulp is now removed from the container and squeezed to remove excess coloring. It can be handled like putty, being placed over armatures or inserted around Vaseline-coated objects to create duplicates. Once dry (usually twenty-four hours later if the room is not damp), the covering is carefully slit with a knife or razor and then peeled away to form two halves. These can serve as molds, into which plaster of Paris may be poured, or they may be glued together to form the duplicate.

Papier-mâché duplicates should be dried at room temperature. If you are impatient, use a low oven heat, but watch the work to prevent scorching. Once dry to the touch, paint the object and then give it a final coat of cut shellac after the paint dries. *Cut shellac* is made with equal parts of shellac and alcohol.

Papier-mâché easter eggs

A popular trick at Easter time is to make eggs out of papier-mâché. Work around the form of a hard-boiled or china egg. When the paper has dried, slice it about the middle with a sharp knife or razor blade to form two halves. Remove the egg form. A strip of paste-soaked paper joins the sections together again. When the egg is decorated, the joint is invisible.

Hand-decorated Easter eggs constructed of papier-mâché and decorated with tempera paints. (*Courtesy Prang Studios*)

A variation of the hollow papier-mâché egg will find much favor with youngsters. Before you seal the halves together again, conceal a small party favor inside, either packed in cotton or left to rattle provocatively.

Eggs can serve as the basic form for many an imaginative little figure. With faces painted on and locks of hair affixed with glue, these make whimsical favors. Add paper hats, gumdrop noses, tinsel wings, or costumes—the possibilities are endless.

Below: Papier-mâché eggs, hand colored with Dek-All paint and laquered for durability. If formed by molding around hard-boiled egg, papier-mâché covering and egg can later be cut in half, contents removed, and hollowed-out object used to hide a party favor. Egg is then joined together with a strip of masking tape and entire outside decorated to hide strip.

Above: Table centerpiece constructed of paper products and hat veiling. Whiskers, ears, eyes, mouth, neckpiece, and basket trim are of colored crepe paper; body is cardboard box covered with wrapping paper and crepe bands. Eggs are papier-mâché wrapped with crepe paper and decorated with colored stickers. *(Courtesy Dennison Manufacturing Company)*

Precisionists can try their hand at traditional spyglass eggs. For this purpose use blown out or papier-mâché eggs. Remove the smaller end to form a peephole and hand decorate the interior. Add tiny props of cotton and colored tinsel, forming a landscape, scenic design, or abstraction. A cellophane window covers the hole, held in place with cake icing. Lace-paper doilies are glued to the base to complete your holiday favor.

Giant paper rabbit made of crepe paper, construction paper, ribbons, and a large grocery sack. What keeps it aloft? A helium-inflated toy balloon hidden inside! If you lack the helium, insert a garden variety of balloon and suspend it from the ceiling on a string. *(Photo: Dennison Manufacturing Company)*

Paper Toys and Games

Don't discard empty milk containers, oatmeal boxes, cardboard egg crates, or candy boxes. These can all be converted into sturdy toy banks. Any hollow cardboard container will do the trick.

Take the trio opposite, for example, created by the Studio of Binney & Smith. "The Barefoot Senorita" is made from an odd-shaped candy box; the tall gentleman with yarn arms is from a mailing tube, and "The Indian Maiden" combines use of a mailing tube and two paper plates. The plates were shaped about a burned-out light bulb, which was then removed, and the two segments were glued together. Bits of corrugated cardboard form her hair. These cardboard banks were painted with tempera and slots were cut on top or in the back to allow insertion of coins. Children will love these gay figures. They can make them without any difficulty.

All three banks were strengthened with a few layers of pasted paper and then painted to cover the stripping. If balancing becomes a problem, just drop a lead weight into the hollowed interior.

Use yarn for hair, papier-mâché for wings, arms, legs, clothing, and the like on other figures. Banks might be made in the form of animals, cowboys, clowns, fat little birds, or angels and devils. For additional decoration, apply a bit of glue and sprinkle on glitter, paste on jelly-bean noses, and use shredded cellophane to simulate feather boas and ruffles.

Toy banks can be made of cardboard boxes, paper plates, and mailing tubes. This gay trio, decorated in tempera paints, uses corrugated board, and yarn for additional trim. Coin slot is cut on back. (*Courtesy Binney and Smith*)

Opposite: A collection of Christmas-tree trimmings made from odds and ends.

Top left: Key coil. Twist metal coil from sardine can and leave key attached. Wind free end around key. After painting gold, cement on sequins and add a gay bow.

Second left: Milkweed dangles. Poke two holes near top of a milkweed pod, using ice pick. Fasten Christmas ball inside pod with fine wire run up through holes. Add ribbon and attach ornament to additional length of the wire.

Center left: Yarn spheres. Inflate a balloon. Soak yarn in flour paste and wind loosely around balloon. Let dry. Deflate and remove balloon. The yarn cage may then be decorated with paint and glitter.

Fourth left: Spike stars. Cut foil paper in 3-inch circles, then cut circles into quarters and roll each into a cone. Fasten with tape. Poke two holes on opposite sides of a ping-pong ball and insert wire to make a hanging loop. Glue on cones and glitter.

Lower left and center: Wallpaper ornaments. Cut motifs from wallpaper samples. Place motif on ¼-inch- or ½-inch-thick Styrofoam sheet, trace edge with sharp pencil, then cut Styrofoam along penciled line on flat surface with sharp knife. Push cut-out motif from Styrofoam sheet. If necessary, cut on other side of Styrofoam to free motif. Using Styrofoam cement, attach wallpaper to Styrofoam cut-out. Use glue and glitter to highlight motifs.

Top center and right: Screen ornaments. Use any fine mesh screen and, for extra sparkle, try the cellophane-impregnated variety. The birdcage (*top center*): Cut two strips of screen 9 inches long by ½ inch wide and make into rings, stapling ends together. Insert one ring through other at right angles to make double ring. Staple at top and bottom. Fringe half an aluminum pie plate, and staple to bottom. (Curl fringe around pencil.) Cut wire 6 inches long and attach around top of ornament where rings intersect, so wires fall between adjacent strips. String wires with beads; attach other beads to bottom of ornament.

Second right: The spiral. Cut screen in narrow strip, wind to form spiral. Staple together at top. Thread fine wire through circles, adding beads between circles. Wire beads to outer circle and add loop for hanging.

Center and lower right: Pipe-cleaner twists. String hollow Christmas beads on pipe cleaners and curve ends to hold. Twist into unusual shapes. Hang with thread. Stars are made of twisted pipe-cleaner lengths pushed through beads. Tree is constructed of same material. (*Courtesy McCall's* Needlework and Crafts Magazine)

Painting a stained-glass window. (*Courtesy* A. *DiDonato*)

Simulated Stained Glass on Paper

Though the making of professional stained glass is an exacting art, requiring skill and knowledge for control, by the use of wax crayons a handsome and simplified technique has been developed. The design shown in color opposite was rendered on heavy wrapping paper.

The first step is, obviously, to select a motif and make a master sketch on tracing paper, breaking it up into a mosaic effect with black lines that imitate leading. This is known as the cartoon. It will be then traced on the working surface or, if plastic sheets or glass are used, be placed underneath so that the freehand painting can be done atop the guide. The theme may be naturalistic, traditional, or abstract. Bold, simple designs are recommended.

Once the motif is transferred or positioned, you are ready to start working.

After tracing your design onto the heavy paper, dip a wad of cotton into oil (mineral oil, baby oil, or cooking oil) and rub it evenly across the surface to impregnate the paper. This will serve two purposes: make the paper translucent and add brilliance to the wax colors. Now, color in your motif with the crayons. Confine the color to each leaded black segment and choose hues that contrast richly and complement each other. Do not try for a gaudy effect; rather, study actual stained glasswork to note the subtlety of placement that is inherent in well-designed examples of this craft.

A rough effect is achieved by freely stroking the crayons across the paper. A purer blending can be accomplished by dipping your crayons

[37]

into the oil between strokes and going over the colors a second time. For deeper hues, turn the paper over and add more crayoning on the reverse.

Experiment if you wish with sgraffito effect by scraping the wax color away with a sharp tool.

When the coloring is completed, a clear lacquer can be sprayed or brushed over both sides of the paper to make it more durable. The panel is then placed over a window and secured with masking tape or the adhesive-backed colored plastic tapes that are available in most department stores and supermarkets.

Silly Masks

Take an empty egg carton, add a few bits of cardboard, decorate with tempera, and there's a delightfully grotesque mask which a child can tie in place with elastic string or simply mount on the wall of his room. The facial features of the masks can be made of egg-divider sections stapled to the container or imbedded in moist pulp. The pulp is made by mixing cleansing tissues (such as Kleenex) with white library paste. They are then positioned as nose, mouth, eyes, and ears, pressed firmly in place, and painted when dry. If they are to be worn, cut out small peepholes in the eyes.

Cardboard masks made of empty egg containers can be worn by children or hung on the wall of a playroom or den. (Photo: Frank J. Brizzi)

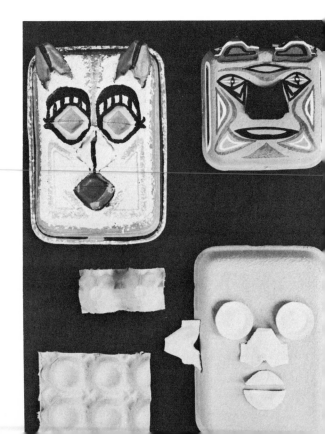

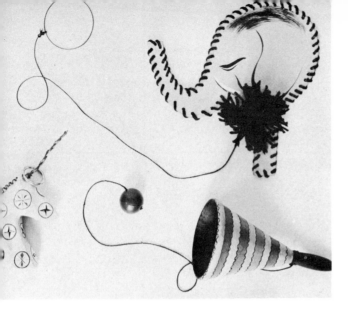

Catch games made of paper products, string, curtain rings, and rubber ball. (*Photo: Frank J. Brizzi*)

Catch Game

Catch games are fun to make, even more fun to use. Several layers of cardboard, thin enough to be cut with scissors, are painted and shellacked, then laced together with string or yarn. An ice pick or paper punch will provide holes through which the lacing may be inserted. A length of string is tied to the handle—of wood or heavy cardboard—and a rubber ball is fastened to its end. (The ball has a hole through it in which the string can be knotted securely. You may simply push a large sewing needle through the rubber and thus insert the string.)

The body of the ball cup is made of a small can or several paper cups stapled together for strength. Attach the handle with adhesive tape. Paint the toy, then shellac it.

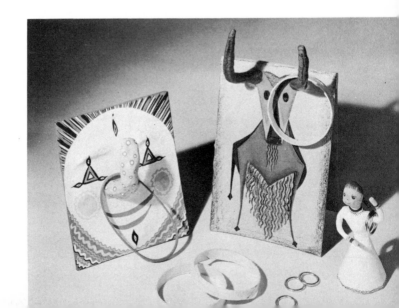

Ring-toss game using papier-mâché targets mounted on heavy cardboard backing. Rings for tossing are empty masking-tape reels, tops of paper drink containers, and brass curtains rings.

The ring toss game is even easier to make. Any papier-mâché object shaped in an animal form will do for the ring catch. Just insert a heavy piece of wire as the target, step back a few feet, and toss curtain rings at it. Or the ring toss may be hand-held. In that case, add a stick handle to the object, attach a long string, and tie the other end of the string to a bracelet, curtain ring, or Mason-jar rubber. Toss the ring into the air and try to catch it as it falls. If you miss, the string will keep the ring from bouncing away on the ground.

Paper Clown and Sort-of-Penguin

These two delightful, three-dimensional abstractions are highly stylized interpretations, showing the high degree of professional skill that can be achieved in making decorative toys. The paper of which they are made is colored with paints and crayons before the cutting, folding, and scoring are done. All that you need are a pair of scissors, stapler, paste, razor blade, and coloring materials. The clown's body is supported by a thin pole of wood or wire thrust up through the body and head. The base is made of cardboard or modeling clay. The bird is papier-mâché.

Paper clown and sort-of-penguin are rainy-day toy projects made of paper. Bird is papier-mâché; clown is white paper that has been painted, then folded, cut out, and scored before being glued together and mounted against wooden or wire pole. Details are of cut paper. (*Courtesy Binney and Smith*)

[40]

Finger Painting

THOSE OF US who are accustomed to thinking of finger painting as a juvenile preoccupation will be surprised to learn that it is an
ancient art and can be of near-infinite delicacy in the right hands. It was
invented some thirteen hundred years ago during China's Tang Dynasty by
the gifted master, Chang Chao. Mr. Chang was a court painter who
abandoned his brushes in favor of his finger tips when he discovered he
could create gossamer-fine lines with a flick of his fingernails. Today,
many professionals follow his procedure and the art is still largely Oriental
in concept and flavor.

For youngsters, however, no such delicacy is pursued; they love to
swirl their palms through the paint and apply it with joyous abandon.
For this reason it is a favorite occupation at the kindergarten and elementary levels.

During the early 1930s Ruth Faison Shaw reintroduced the forgotten
technique and its popularity has zoomed to the point where few introductory art classes have not explored its wonderful possibilities for in-
stilling rhythm and freehand expression in their neophyte Michelangelos.

The majority of paintings are, obviously, abstractions; but for more
advanced practitioners it is a challenging medium for depicting landscapes,
flowers, animals, and other natural forms.

1   2

No prior art training is necessary to enjoy this method—indeed, thinking in terms of technique is something of a drawback at first. One of the best ways to finger-paint is while listening to music, just letting yourself go as the mood suggests.

Commercial paints are manufactured for finger painting and they are low in cost. Both Binney & Smith and American Crayon Company offer excellent kits. It is also possible to make your own paints by mixing powdered tempera with liquid laundry starch. Another method is to mix wallpaper paste and water to creamlike consistency and then add powdered tempera or its premixed equivalent, poster paint. The least expensive paint of all is produced in the following manner:

1. Mix ½ cup laundry starch with ½ cup of cold water.
2. Pour in 1 quart of boiling water, stirring to paste.
3. Add ½ cup of tempera paint or powder tempera. Mix thoroughly. Then, to preserve the paint, add 2 tablespoons of sodium benzoate, if desired. The paint may then be stored in jars or tin cans with lids.

Painting is done on a smooth paper stock; any glazed type will prove satisfactory, and paper is also available commercially for this technique. Beginners on a modest budget can even use smooth wrapping paper.

Finger painting is a damage-free medium; no matter how enthusiastically you splash around, the color can be easily washed away with water. We recommend that the painter don old clothes and spread newspapers or oilcloth over the working table. Even if you are bedridden, there's no reason why you can't put on an apron, roll up your sleeves, and plunge into the creative project.

3   4

1. With a sponge wet sheet of smooth art paper on both sides. Work is done while paper is moist. 2. To make finger paint, pour liquid starch onto paper until it forms a pool about half-dollar size. On this, drop ½ teaspoon of powder tempera paint, and mix. 3. Actual finger painting is begun after mixture is spread over entire paper. 4. Using side of hand, clenched fist, and fingers, start painting freely and rapidly.

The procedure is quite simple; start by wetting both sides of the paper thoroughly with a sponge and smooth away wrinkles and air bubbles with your palm, working from the center outward. Then, just dip your fingers and palms in the paint and begin! You can apply a ground coat of solid hue, allow it to dry, and paint on top of this with varying colors. Dark colors will show up more prominently, so use these first, creating swirls, circles, squares—whatever you wish. Delicate details can be added by using the edge of your fingers and your fingernails. Work lightly and do not scratch the paper surface.

For beginners, the palette of colors should be limited at first, until the basic idea is understood. Select a rich brown or purple for a ground, then one or two lighter colors for overpainting. Remember, all mixing is done directly on the paper, not by putting the thick paints together. For this reason, it is often exciting to swirl on the colors quickly and add others while the earlier ones are still wet. A finger painting will dry in just a few minutes.

Finger paint colors mix, but your palette should be limited at first to avoid having overlapping paints turn into a neutral mud.

The completed work is not very permanent. After some time it may flake in spots; and, if water is applied, retouching the surface can create streaks.

But it's lots of fun. Everything is freehand. No tracing or sketching is logical. Work fast and generously; and, when a design is achieved, stop at once. It is tempting to continue splashing about, but this will only result in scrubbing away what might have been a worthwhile design.

3
_____

Collages and Appliqué

Collage, as the name suggests, is a collection of odds and ends, brought together and mounted on a flat surface to create a design.

There is no limit to the assortment of materials you can use to form a collage: rags, buttons, paint, threads, photographs, bits of wood, and so on.

A collage is usually abstract rather than literal; it does not attempt to portray something in a lifelike manner. Rather, it distills the meaning of an object, a theme, or a composition, reducing this meaning to secondary importance. The greatest emphasis is on the beauty of the created design and the excitement caused by these seemingly unrelated things being brought together to make a single, related composition.

One of the simplest attacks to this problem is in the use of colored bits of paper, scraps torn from newspapers, illustrations from magazines, and perhaps a bit of pen or brush work. For example, let's suppose you wish to create a collage that emphasizes a definite theme: "Hollywood, U.S.A." How would you go about symbolizing this theme? Well, you might start with a bulletin board on which to mount your collage. Then,

Opposite: "Annunciation." Collage by Margaret Moroney, made w scraps of colored paper and newsprint. The drawing of faces, han and feet was added last.

It is
ch phase ...graphy
to spec... z ... may
rait wo... ... nay
ws or ... ... otograp...
which you choose, chemi...
art will be helpful and...
specialized training in a...
...ol is practically indispe...
...ner, without training, is
...or such odd jobs as helping
...ment, clean-up and legwork
...excellent method of breaki...
...eld and learning the mecha...
...ve an apprenticeship for tw...
...ears under a skilled photograph...
... Deschin's "Opportunities
...aphy" contains useful vocationa...
...ion. It can be obtained from Vo-
...Guidance Manuals, Inc., 45 West
...New York 19, New York (Price
... perhaps you can find a copy
...al library.
...ately, the market is flood...
...raphers at present he...
...mber who rec...
...War I...

choosing objects with meaning suggestive of the motion-picture industry, begin to assemble the collage. Among the possible fragments: torn newspaper review of a motion picture, strip of film, theater tickets, lipstick cases and powder puffs, a number of torn-out pages from a movie magazine, popcorn, and a background of painted or pasted stars. These are the props. They must be organized as a single design. When this is done, the result is a collage.

While a collage is primarily a two-dimensional project, it is possible to add a degree of depth too, since some of the materials may have thickness up to possibly a half inch or so. Avoid applying heavy objects merely for the sake of being clever. Halves of wax fruit, for example, are not nearly so effective as would be colored paper cutouts to suggest these same halves of fruit. Keep your collage relatively flat.

For the serious student or artist, there is no better way to explain space composition than by collage, which challenges you to arrange planes and colored textures in a manner that is exciting to view.

Suggestions to Parents and Teachers

If you'd like to try your youngsters at collage, make the themes simple and the materials equally basic. Keep scraps to small size so that excessive use of scissors is avoided. Bear in mind that a collage is not only to look at but also to feel. Children love to touch things, and a collage will introduce them to creative art more effectively than almost any other medium.

Choose materials for their feel. Include bits of cotton (soft), sandpaper (rough), ribbon (sleek), cellophane (crinkly—and noisy too!).

A simple first project might be: "The Sky above Me." Against a large sheet of blue composition paper, the small-fry artist arranges cotton tuft clouds, colored adhesive stars (the kind you use for keeping good-conduct charts), planets made of colored paper circles, and perhaps a sea shell or two (to suggest the ringed planet, Saturn). The sun can be a brilliant yellow cellophane circle or several cellophane drinking straws tied about the middle and fanned out to imitate a sunburst.

Another juvenile theme: "A Visit to the Farm." Here you can make your selection of props from leaves, cutout barns of red construction paper, cellophane packing excelsior (the kind florists and gift shops use to protect their wares and make a soft nest), which makes wonderful grass for a farmyard, and rolling hills too when pasted down. The farm animals may be paper cutouts (yellow for pigs, brown and white for cows, red for chickens, and so on) or those little yarn animals available at five-and-tens for decorating gift packages or used as place settings around Eastertime. Again, the sun can be cellophane circles or a cellophane straw sunburst. If it is wintertime, the ground may be covered with cotton snow.

Above: a collection of scrap materials is stored in cartons by the artist, Chris Jones. *Right:* shells, driftwood, coral, and chicken wire suggest a collage with a nautical theme. (*Courtesy* People and Places)

Materials for Collage

A basic list of materials for collage-making would probably include: newspaper, pipe cleaners, sandpaper, toothpicks, wood shavings, cellophane, metallic papers, yarn, wrapping (gift) papers, pine cones and needles, cellophane grass, corks, cotton, straws, colored papers, tinfoil, feathers, fabric scraps, bobby pins, birthday candles, sequins, fish tank pebbles, and straws from a broom.

Scrap-Pile Collage

Murals and decorative panels—made entirely of junk, flotsam, and bits of discarded materials! And they are professional in appearance; so professional, indeed, that Chris Jones, a former fashion model, has made them the basis of a well-paying enterprise. She has turned her imagination loose on a motley collection of broken glass, empty coconut husks, sea shells, rusty spades, and other indescribable jetsam. Pictures of her and some of her work are shown on these pages.

A walk down any beach is certain to turn up the weathered bric-a-brac which is raw material for junk murals. Poking around in your attic is also rewarding. When you've come back from a treasure hunt of this sort, the loot is deposited in cartons to await cleaning, sanding, and painting. Then, a theme is developed.

What theme? This is where imagination plays a major role. What does your treasure chest contain? What does it suggest to you? To Miss Jones, who parlayed scraps of fabric, an old bottle, and a weatherbeaten spade into a pirate mural, it resulted in a profitable sale to a Florida yachting club. Her murals now feature such unlikely items as old phonograph records, fish bones, chicken feet, and automobile gaskets! These are arranged on sheets of plywood to form a decorative design, then stapled or glued in position. Finally, the panel is framed and another scrap pile masterpiece is ready.

The tools for this type of project are to be found in any household; ruler, stapler, hammer, perhaps a drill and tin snips. As in any handicraft project, a rough idea is sketched, then the layout is refined to take advantage of the shapes, textures, and colors of the scrap materials. The items are then positioned against the plywood sheet, studied for effect, and finally fastened permanently. Anything goes in completing the panel; usually a few lines in paint help establish any features for which appropriate scraps are not on hand. But the less actual artwork that is required, the better. That's part of the fun—finding scraps that will do the job.

How Two Murals Were Made

Pirate Panel.

Headpieces are dress scraps and a discarded felt hat to which gold ribbon has been sewed. Shirts are rags. Belt buckle is an automobile gasket from a junkyard. The leering eyes of the pirate trio are discards from old toys and are far more appropriate in these murals than in the hands (and mouths) of youngsters. No self-respecting buccaneer would be caught dead without an earring. You can make these of tightly coiled wire, big brass curtain rings, or costume jewelry. The hair is made of steel wool, stapled in position, and of black-coated, heavily insulated electric wire. The hair on the fabric-derived chests is once again steel wool, this time glued in place. Other props consist of an old garden spade—the rustier the better—an empty wine bottle, large knife, and a few yards of twisted dress fabric, for bandannas. Facial features are created by bending coat hangers or heavy gauge wire, and the flesh is represented by cutout strips of burlap, cork, or lining fabric.

To carry out the motif, the mural has been bordered with heavy hemp rope and bamboo. Bits of corrugated cardboard will do nicely to suggest corduroy clothing, if desired, and a ragged shirt can prove a handy prop.

[48]

Chris Jones and her three Buccaneer friends whom she created out of odds and ends. The collage is now permanently displayed at the Biscayne Bay Yachting Club. (*Photo: Bill Kobrin*)

Rooster Panel.

What could be more appropriate for designing a strutting rooster's body than snips of chicken wire? The comb of the fowl is made from a piece of bright red fabric or dish washing sponge, and the tail is a plume from an old hat. Add to this a pair of authentic chicken feet and—*voilà!* there's your rooster. (See illustration on page 44.)

Each part of the panel is affixed to a background base of plywood or composition board with small nails or staples. A simple picture, ready for hanging in a playroom, den, or bar. The same procedure is easily adapted for other stylized panels, made of commonplace scraps, yet, when assembled, having a fresh and unusual appearance. You can try bird panels, fish forms, landscapes too. Just remember to select scraps that are in some way related to the subject—feathers for birds; dried ferns, waxed leaves, twigs, and flat stones (glued or stapled in position) for landscapes and barnyard scenes.

Keep your backgrounds simple and try to avoid adding any painted scenic effects. The idea is to assemble and design the scrap-pile murals, not to make a painting.

[49]

"Birds of My Childhood." Embroidered appliqué design by Eve Peri.

Appliqué Technique

The collage effect can be translated to the medium of fabric; and, when bits of cloth are cut out and sewed onto a neutral background, this is known as appliqué. The commonest form of appliqué is quilts, aprons, and decorative clothing. You can also combine the paper and assorted scrap materials type of collage with appliqué to create abstracted murals and pictures.

The initial step in planning an appliqué is to sketch a design, then trace it onto cardboard, working full size. Around the edges of this design rule in a penciled border approximately a quarter inch larger than the outermost extreme of the motif on all sides. This allows for a border on the fabric to which you will transfer your design, permitting it to be turned under at the edges.

You are now ready to trace the motif onto your bits of variously colored fabrics. Once this is done, the bits are cut out with scissors, allowing a quarter inch all around. Iron flat to eliminate wrinkles. They are now ready to sew onto the neutral background material. The pieces must be basted to prevent unraveling. This is accomplished by folding under the edges for a quarter inch. Circular areas may be snipped slightly every half inch or so to allow for turning evenly. Once the appliqué bits are positioned and basted, sew them in place, using thread that matches the fabric and employing a blind stitch, which shows a minimum of thread. Sew down through the background and through both layers of the folded-under edging.

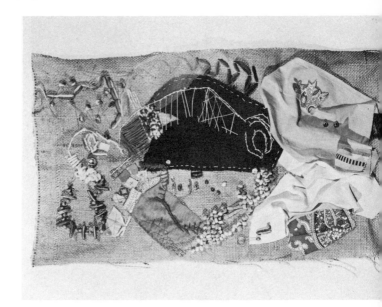

A modern collage designed by Rosalia Aquado, combining scraps of fabric, beads, and yarn stitched onto a piece of burlap bag.

"Persian Moon," an abstract appliqué design by Eve Peri.

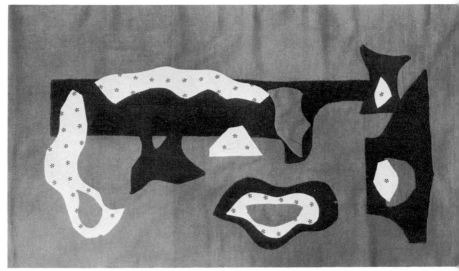

4

Fantastic Celastic

THOSE WHO LIKE to experiment with new art mediums will certainly want to try Celastic, also known as Sculpt-o-Fab, a versatile material which may, in time, supplant papier-mâché, at least from the practical standpoint of the serious craftsman and display artist.

With Celastic you can create exact duplicates of just about any solid object in a matter of minutes! Stagecrafters, display artists, and educators speak in enthusiastic terms about this unusual, colloid-treated fabric which clings to masonry, plaster casts, valuable original sculpture, trees, rocks—and, when lifted away, becomes a durable "double."

Now you can make your own duplicates of expensive museum pieces at a cost that is far less than for plaster casts. You can, in fact, make low-cost molds from which many more duplicates in plaster will emerge. Celastic is no mere mechanical tool. It has a host of creative uses in the hands of imaginative artists. The material comes in two types: in sheet form, for reproducing objects that are to be covered completely, and in strips for freehand shaping and "scribble sculpture."

Basically, Celastic is a tough cotton fabric that has been impregnated by the manufacturer with a colloidal plastic. When dipped in a special softening agent, it becomes pliable and can be draped, molded, or shaped by hand. It dries rock hard in about twenty minutes, becoming a weatherproof substance that can be drilled, sanded, cut, or painted.

Celastic (Sculpt-o-Fab) mask is decorated with flat colors
and bright strips of cellophane tape. Hat and neckpiece are of same material. (*Courtesy Binney and Smith*)

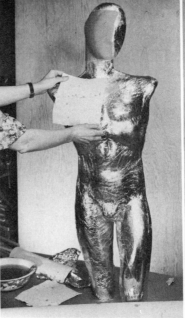
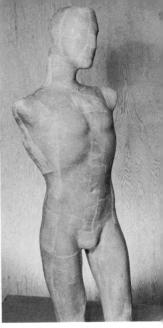

1   2   3

Making a sculpture duplicate takes about two hours. 1. Parting agent is wiped c brushed over original piece, making later removal of tin foil simple. 2. Tin foil i applied over original sculpture to act as separator. 3. Swatches of softened Celastic an now applied over the tin foil. Areas may overlap for, when dry, seams are practical

Industry has found countless uses for it. Hollywood sets are made of it, for it is low in cost, takes abuse, and is extremely lightweight. The automotive people use it for patching holes, torn fenders, and weather-eroded parts. Even the orthopedics industry has found it useful for making artificial limbs and braces.

Are you a model enthusiast? Shape it into tunnels, landscaping, and miniature bridges for your train sets. Make toy planes, dolls, fashion mannequins, stage props of it. You name it and it can be made of Celastic.

For casting, Celastic can create positive or negative molds. Freehand projects are child's play. You simply dip the material in the softener, wait a few minutes until it is semidry, then shape it into flowers, abstractions, or simulated drapery. It hardens quickly. If you wish to reshape it or make corrections, just immerse it once more in the softener and work it over again.

Celastic can be adapted to silk-screen work so that the finished project is no longer confined to flat planes or simple curves. For example, you can apply a silk-screened motif of a man's head on a flat sheet of the material before dipping it in the softener. Then, with a few deft touches of your fingers you tilt the nose up, puff out the cheeks, and round the

[54]

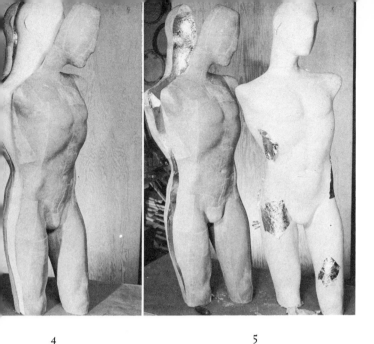

4

5

invisible. 5. After twenty minutes the shell is slit down back and the halves are peeled off. Original object may now be removed and the two halves joined with strips of softened Celastic. 5. Original model (*right*) and Celastic duplicate.

Celastic stripping is run through a pan of special softener, then curled or scribbled into freeform shapes. It dries quickly and weighs very little, making it useful for making props, displays, mannequins, duplicates, and masks. Here it is being curled and twisted into a negative mold to make a mannequin form like the one at top left of picture.

brow. Is your motif a ballerina? Slit the outline and flare her skirt, three dimensionally. Lift up the leg and bend the body to any desired position. She will seem to step right out of the display! You are now working in a brand new medium—silk-screen sculpture.

If your school or amateur group has a small budget for props, Celastic is one answer. Just cover fruit, window boxes, architectural columns, frames, masks, cornices, helmets with this material and, when it dries, free the object by slitting with a knife. Peel away the two sections from the original and join the halves together with strips of Celastic to create a duplicate. When these joining strips dry, the patch becomes almost invisible and the entire duplicate will take paint or shellac readily.

Paper-Sculpture Technique

Here is the working procedure for all those projects that you previously constructed of papier-mâché.

1. Cut pattern from Celastic sheeting and dip into softening bath for a few seconds. Lay the pattern flat on a table and allow it to set for about fifteen minutes. When it is slightly tacky and feels like wet leather, it is ready for shaping. While it dries out a bit, keep lifting it every few minutes from the tabletop to prevent sticking.

2. Now you can shape, twist, or roll it as desired. For textural effects, press the surface against anything having a raised grain or design while still tacky. You may also tool it. For more complicated shapes, use tacks, staples, or masking tape to hold it temporarily in position. After it sets, remove these fasteners. Make any corrections by moistening the area with softener and then reworking. In twenty minutes the object will be rock hard and can then be painted, drilled, sanded, or otherwise decorated.

Casting with Celastic

Initial projects should be simple ones, until you master the technique. Whenever possible, apply Celastic in one piece to avoid later sanding of joints. If the casting mold is deep, tear the material into pieces and apply inside. No paste is necessary; the pieces will cling together when moistened with softener.

Use only a raw plaster mold. Dampen it with water and then brush on the manufacturer's Parting Agent No. 737, a special liquid made for this purpose. This takes the place of the Vaseline or wax usually used for case separation. A word of caution: in casting work, do not apply Celastic to shellacked, waxed, or painted molds, for the parting agent is not made for such work. Instead, use the sheets of tin foil which are described in the illustrated steps for duplicating plaster casts or originals.

[56]

Still life composition created entirely of Celastic.

Full Round Models in Plasteline or Clay

If you are working with a Plasteline or Milo model, tear sheets of Celastic and wrap them mummy-fashion about the original until it is entirely covered. When the Celastic dries, cut it from the clay figure with a sharp knife and remove the original from the two halves. Then join the sections with more strips or sheets of Celastic.

Materials and Equipment

Metal pan for holding softening agent. (Keep covered when not in use to prevent evaporation.)

Clothesline or rack on which to place moistened sheets for drying.

Oilcloth table cover to protect desk's working surface.

Stapling gun.

A pair of rubber gloves. The softener is not injurious under normal working conditions, but it does dry like rubber cement and should be removed from fingers to prevent this from caking.

Source of Supplies

Celastic and its attendant materials are available from the national distributor: Ben Walters, Inc., 156 Seventh Avenue, New York 11, N.Y.

Celastic ribbon comes in three widths: 3/16 inch, 3/4 inch, and 1 inch.

The sheeting comes in several widths and weights; and, for large-scale use, rolls of twenty-five and fifty yards are also available, with prices scaled very much lower than for single sheets.

5

Ink Decorating

Things with Strings

YOU CAN CREATE unusual designs simply by drawing with a piece of string dipped in ink. The effects are quite unpredictable, but a pressed string print takes less than a minute to complete. The cost is obviously small—a few drops of ink and a few sheets of typewriter paper will do the job. Here's the procedure:

1. Spread newspapers over a worktable and place a smooth sheet of cardboard on top to act as the work surface.

2. Pour a quantity of ink into a dish. (If desired, you may prepare several dishes of ink of varying colors, for it is probable that you will want to superimpose one color on top of another, after you master the simple technique.)

3. Into the ink dish goes a length of string—about two feet in length will prove most satisfactory. Saturate the string with ink, then blot it somewhat with newspaper until it is moist, but not loaded.

4. Place a sheet of white typewriter paper (or any similar stock) on your worktable, then dangle the string across it, letting it curl and twist into an interesting design. Drop it in place with one end trailing down toward you and off the paper. Now, put a second sheet of paper on top, making a sandwich of the string.

5. Put a magazine or any large, lightweight article of the same general shape on top of the paper and press down evenly with the ball of your hand. This will establish the string design on the paper. If you wish to stop at this point, you will have a simple blotted design of predetermined pattern and its mirror image on the second sheet of paper. But, if you want to play our string game, the unpredictable part still lies ahead.

6. Now, lightly hold the magazine in place and grasp the trailing edge of the string with your other hand. Then begin to pull it. Work slowly, tugging the string down, then sideways—any direction you wish, just so you keep changing direction as the string comes away. When the entire string has been removed, examine the results on your two pieces of paper. They will be almost exact duplicates, with the top one in reverse.

What do the ink paintings resemble? Pure abstractions? Strange shapes that hint at stories to be told? As with making ink blots, string designs allow the viewer wild flights of fancy in interpreting the results. An enjoyable party game, but one with valid design possibilities.

When one color has dried or been blotted, you can repeat the procedure on top with another string, dipped in a different color of ink or tempera paint. You may also emphasize certain areas with freehand drawing if you are storytelling and need to point up the subject for easier recognition.

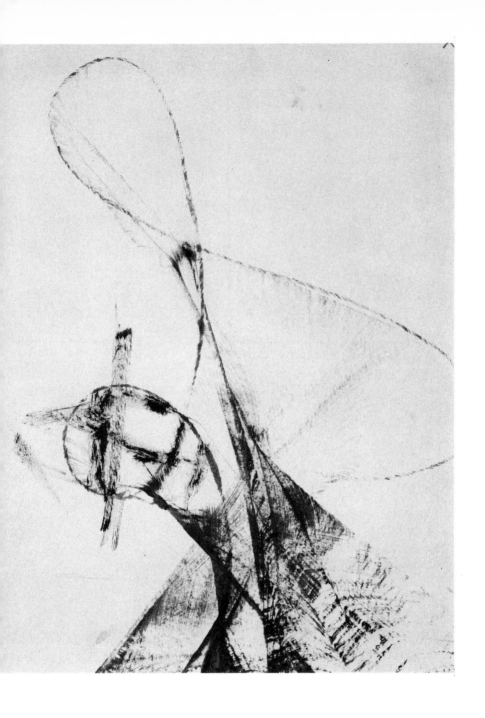

"Gaucho with Lasso" design made with string and ink.

String and ink pattern adapted as a book-jacket design.

Ink-Blot Art

What do you see when you look at abstract blots of ink? Generations of children have played the ink-blot game and, some time ago, it was given further dignity by the psychology researcher, emerging as a widely used test for interpreting human behavior. Any way you look at it, ink-blot art is entertainment. Moreover, the technique has been adapted for many decorative purposes, including framed wall panels, lampshades, playroom and office murals, and, most important of all from the artist's standpoint, as a source of inspiration for decorative designs.

As an example of the serious use to which the ink blot is being put, examine the "Kaleidoscroll" reproduced in this chapter. These fascinating wall hangings are entirely hand rendered, using a palette of India inks, and white tempera for accentuation and a feeling of texture. The inks are black, orange, turquoise, yellow, and brown. The stock is ordinary charcoal rendering paper of tan-gray color. Each motif is an original, made by applying the ink spatters after the paper has been folded once vertically. The inks are added one at a time, directly on or close to the fold. The paper is then refolded and the artist's fingers are pressed along the fold. As the ink is forced haphazardly in every direction, the paper is opened and examined. Then, the next color or colors will be dropped where they will blend most effectively. While the technique is accidental, it is quite possible to control the general flow and build up a motif. Inks may be allowed to dry completely before the next color is applied, or they they can be blended while still wet to produce additional hues and subtle shadings.

The Kaleidoscrolls are then mounted on Masonite or wallboard, with a contrasting border of glued paper or plastic adhesive, and a hanging eyelet is affixed to the back. The samples are the handiwork of Bruce Hill.

The ink-blot doodles shown here are the result of a between-classes session by a group of art teachers at Columbia University. At first the blots were purely accidental. Then, someone saw the shape of a Scottie terrier in one, and another teacher, standing at the opposite side of the desk, thought it resembled a French poodle instead. It was discovered that viewing it upside down produced the entirely different description. From this start, it wasn't long before the coffee break turned into a parlor game. Producing the blots proved only half the fun; thinking up appropriate titles became a challenge.

A few pointers on blot printing: First, choose a slightly absorbent paper. Then, fold it once before printing. Drip ink with a medicine dropper (or

Ink blot designs.

Kaleidoscroll is an unusual adaptation of the folded-ink-blot technique —made by designer Bruce Hill. Each item is an original, rendered in inks and opaque tempera. Designs are on thin paper mounted onto white board backings. *(Courtesy Peter Pepper Products)*

the stopper of the ink bottle) sparingly, working at first along the folded line. Two or three drops at a time will suffice. Fold again on the original line and lightly press with your finger tips. A heavier pressure with the flat of the hand will cover greater area; but, for delicate traceries, work gingerly. Examine your blot picture frequently. You can even develop a picture deliberately by adding a few touches and lines for emphasis. If color (or black ink) is to be added wet-in-wet to other colors, plan your design so the second color creates a harmonious hue when intermixed. Red ink on top of yellow, for example, produces subtle tones of orange; a bit of blue ink also added on top of these will turn in brownish-purple. Textural effects are achieved by adding opaque tempera colors. You can also dip string in the inks or tempera and dangle it across the blot, thus combining a symmetrical design with a freely abstracted linear element.

Finally, you may use the colored ink-blot picture as a background and then draw more literally across this with tempera or India ink. Some beautiful effects are possible in this way.

[64]

6

Styrofoam

You've seen this new art material used commercially for making window displays, and it lends itself admirably to a host of creative ideas.

Styrofoam looks like snow, is delightfully tactile, visually exciting, and light as a feather. Manufacturers of display materials are a source of supply; so are florist supply houses and hobby shops, and you can often get it in department and dime stores. The cost is moderate.

What can you do with Styrofoam? This low-density polystyrene product is ideal for sculpture and carving projects. You can cut it with a knife, razor blade, or band saw.

Using Styrofoam, you can form the elements of a mobile, create abstract shapes, snowmen, and snowballs for holiday centerpieces, even use decorated blocks of it as a catch-all for holding your pens, pencils, brushes, and other art tools. (Simply poke the objects into the block and they'll stand ready for instant use. Be sure the block is adhered to a heavy base, though; the Styrofoam is so light that a two-foot cube of it weighs just a few ounces.)

Adhering Styrofoam to other surfaces, or two pieces together, is best done with Du Pont's Elva-Set, a special emulsion created expressly for the purpose. Ordinary household glues will dissolve Styrofoam. Another way to join pieces of the material together is with toothpicks.

Styrofoam should be carved gently. Being practically all air bubbles, it is not meant for rough use. Make sure your knife is sharp.

Parents and schoolteachers have really found a friend in this new medium. Cutout forms may be combined with painted backgrounds to create three-dimensional posters. White Styrofoam letters provide striking contrast against a dark background.

Do you like to work puppets? Heads made of Styrofoam are easy to carve, and several can be interchanged quickly on the same puppet body simply by making a collar of Styrofoam, cementing it to the puppet neck, and then temporarily fixing the head to this base with a few toothpicks.

White Styrofoam can be colored by spraying it with water color or tempera. Use an insect spray gun for the purpose, never a brush. Dek-All, Tempera, and Prang Vinyl Art Colors may be used to decorate Styrofoam.

Another decorative idea: you can purchase Styrofoam in cylindrical lengths, even as huge canes. Just wrap bright ribbons along the canes to create a candy peppermint effect for Christmas decorations and party favors.

A charming Christmas centerpiece using a Styrofoam base and Styrofoam rocks sprinkled with artificial snow. The clever arrangement of Santa and his reindeer is by Julia Berrall. *(Photo: Roche)*

Opposite: Styrofoam figures for a Christmas centerpiece. Small tree balls are used for noses, other details are metallic papers and paint. *(Courtesy Daniel Firestone)*

7

Soapcraft

Soap and Crayon Carving

Nothing seems as useless as the broken bits of soap that remain to gum up your basin—unless it could be the equally valueless stubs of wax crayons that Junior leaves all over the living-room rug. But, wait! They've a creative use after all.

The soap scraps are dumped into a tin can and placed on a hot plate until they melt. The mixture is constantly stirred to prevent smoldering. The smaller the chips or flakes, the quicker they will melt. As the soap melts, bits of crayon are added to impart the desired color. You can choose a single hue or even mix several together. Experimentation will show the proper amount to be used to reach a desired shade. A good substitute for crayons is powder tempera. Pour each color into separate containers—paper cups or milk containers.

It is not necessary to wait for the small bits of soap to melt completely before taking the pan off the heat. Irregular chunks can add a pleasing textural quality, particularly if they are of a contrasting color.

Here's a representative list of sculptural forms that can be attempted by the hobbyist or art student: animals, birds, heads and figures, fish, abstractions.

The cooled block of material is then placed on the worktable (protected by newspapers) and the carving made with an X-acto knife or

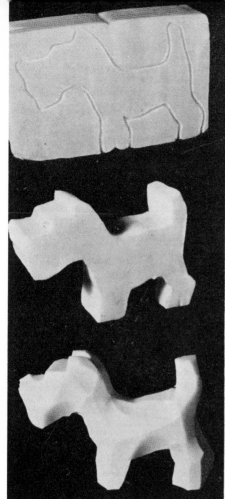
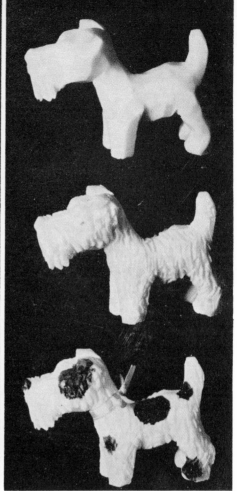

From Lester Gaba's book *Soap Carving*.

Six steps in carving a soap dog. Make outline drawing on one side and two ends of bar of soap, then slowly and carefully whittle soap away from edges, using a sharp pocket knife. Brace thumb against soap as you would when paring fruit. Wiggles in soap, suggesting hair, are made with point of knife. Markings are painted on soap after carving is completed.

razor blade. Fine details can be rendered with a nail file or orange stick. Preliminary sketches may be scratched onto the surface by pressing hard through the paper sketch with a pencil. You will, of course, be dealing with a three-dimensional object, so plan your sketch as a wrap-around. When the actual carving has been done, harsh lines can be softened by rubbing with the finger tips.

Because the soap crayon mixture is soft, it is also possible to shape it with pressure of your fingers.

[69]

Soapsuds Art

Everyone can have a white Christmas inside the house, regardless of what the weatherman predicts outside. All you need is a box of ordinary household detergent or powdered soap and a mixer to turn out the fluffiest snowfall this side of the North Pole.

Jack Frost's secret formula is really no secret at all. Just pour a cupful of packaged soap or detergent into a mixing bowl, add a little water and beat to the consistency of a super stiff meringue. Presto! A huge mound of fresh-fallen snow that can be molded into a fantastic variety of decorative items.

Let's make snowballs first. Roll up your sleeves and grab a handful of soap fluff. Pack it just as you would regular snow. Place the soap snow balls on a bread board to dry. When they harden they'll be permanent. If you'd like to turn them into tree ornaments, press sprigs of mistletoe into them, poke a string or ribbon into the center while they are still moist, pack a little more fluff around the base, and, when it dries, up it goes on the tree!

How about a centerpiece nest to hold a pile of tree globes? (Remove the ornaments and you can use the nest to hold a Christmas punch bowl.) The snow is packed inside a cardboard circle until it hardens.

Children will delight in adding snow to the branches of the tree with this versatile medium. Dip a wooden spoon into the mixture and lightly pat it along the foliage. The same technique will decorate windowpanes with that Jack-Frost-was-here look and will add interest to wreaths and pine boughs.

Opposite: From packaged soap powder and water (beaten with egg beater) tree ornaments can be made in shapes like snowballs and stars which will dry hard. Metal glitter adds sparkle. *Right:* A snowdrift of suds makes a sparkling nest for Christmas-tree ornaments. Same centerpiece can serve as a holder for an eggnog punch bowl. *Below:* Snow suds can also be used to dress up store-bought tree ornaments and to add "frost" to windowpanes.

One of the nicest things about soap snowballs is that they can be packed away with the other ornaments after Christmas and used again and again throughout the years.

Let's make a gay snow tree. First, twist the form out of chicken wire, constructing a cone. Then, using your spatula, build up a thick covering of beaten suds. While the tree is still damp, press in bits of hard candy, small ornaments, gold and silver balls, gumdrops, and candy canes. Use it as your table centerpiece during Christmas dinner. Later it can be placed on the mantel.

Tired of the garden variety of white snow? How about a rainbow assortment of snowballs and other decorations? Just pour a few drops of food coloring in the soap-and-water mixture before beating. (Or use this for painting designs on the hardened snow.) Glitter can also be sprinkled over the shapes and lettering while the soap is still moist.

And to cap it all, let's make a snowy Christmas star for the top of the tree. Cut out a star from cardboard, cover it with the soap snow, garnish with sequins and glitter, and up it goes. There is every opportunity for creativity here, and it's all clean fun.

Snowtree table centerpiece. Decorations pressed into hardened suds consist of hard candies, little gold and silver balls, and cookies. A quartet of candy canes are placed on top.

Pennsylvania German pottery hen. Eighteenth century.

8

Claycraft Decorating and Ceramic Sculpture

C LAY, one of the most common substances taken from the earth, was naturally among the first ever to be fashioned into useful and decorative objects. We have unearthed pottery from civilizations long buried and forgotten. Properly hardened and treated, the clay artifacts you create today probably will last for centuries.

Types of Clay for Modeling

Clay is abundant; there are few localities where you cannot take a shovel and dig up your own modeling medium. It is also inexpensive—so much so that it is often foolish economy to spade and clean it yourself. The quality is not uniform. It is better to purchase modeling clay from a dealer. Being packaged under a trade name, the quality will inevitably be high and the cost still moderate enough. An additional advantage: manufactured clays come in many colors.

If you are planning to use freshly dug clay, it must be treated before working it. All grit, dirt, and loose shale must be removed. Forty-mesh brass screen (called *strainer cloth*) can be bought at a hardware store and stretched on a wooden frame. Then, your clay, mixed with water to a moderately thin consistency (called "slip" by potters), is poured through the mesh to remove impurities. If the clay is not thin enough to pour, force it through the screen by hand. Allow it to settle in a container which you have placed below, so that the water remains on top and the clay is at the bottom. Pour away the water; and your clay, after a slight drying period, will be ready to use. Wrap it in wet burlap and store in a cool place, preferably inside a tin canister.

Those hobbyists who work in large scale, or teachers who plan to do clay projects with an entire class, will find a twenty-gallon garbage pail a good storage container. It will hold two hundred pounds of clay. If you are using clay powder, dilute it with water in a ratio of four parts clay to one of water. Allow this mixture to stand a day or two and it will become uniformly moist.

Plastacine clay may be used for modeling without the need for firing. An oil base has been added to keep it pliable.

Unfired clay pieces are left to dry out when the modeling is completed. They may then be painted with tempera or quick-drying enamel paints. Incising of decoration may also be done on unfired clay before it dries, using any sharp tool or blunted object. Do your painting after firing or, if you use Dek-All, you may paint first, then fire in a 350° oven for a half hour.

Another treatment is to apply a coat of shellac to this clay. This will also serve as a base upon which to apply colored poster paints. Add enough water to the poster paint to help the color stick to the shellac. Another coat of shellac will then make the color permanent. Shellac cannot be successfully used on potter's clay.

Impromptu Kilns

Any work worthy of keeping should be fired. This consists of heat treatment in an oven. The ceramist has many names for this oven, depending on how he uses it, but the most popularly accepted term is kiln.

Firing clay objects is such an interesting process that every ceramist should have a kiln at his disposal. Good-sized electric kilns are available for under $100, new, and can be purchased second hand for a great deal less.

You can, however, make an impromptu kiln without spending a penny. It may not be portable or permanent, but it will do the job quite efficiently. The simplest kiln is constructed by digging a hole in the ground, or punching holes in a large metal trash drum. First, put your unfired clay object on a shelf made of a few bricks, protecting the clay from injury by poking metal rods about it in cagelike fashion, and then heaping wood about the clay. Start a fire and the clay will be fired hard. The obvious disadvantage to this method is the poor control of heat, resulting in uneven firing. But it *is* a time-honored method, practiced now as it has been for centuries, by primitive peoples.

A bit further advanced is the outdoor kiln built of materials which cost around eight or nine dollars. It is made of fire bricks with a sheet of metal for a floor. The bricks are cemented boxlike and the front center is left open as a door. Before fastening a second sheet of metal for the top, a grillwork of iron rods is placed a few inches from the floor. This will serve as a rack to hold your objects. Then, wood or coal is heaped in a hole underneath the kiln, dug into the ground with a vent for a chimney. The metal floor conducts the heat upward rather evenly, and the top metal sheet reflects it down. Aluminum foil can be placed along the walls inside the firing chamber, to help reflect the heat evenly to all sides.

A third type of low-cost, improvised kiln for outdoor use is constructed with nothing more than a drain tile and some stones. Small clay objects are placed inside the curved walls of the tile, lying flat; and both ends are then blocked with stones (or sheets of aluminum foil). This makes an even-temperatured firing chamber. Raise it from the ground a few inches by propping it on stones or bricks, build a coal fire underneath, and your kiln is in operation.

With all of the foregoing types of improvised kilns, there is no exact way to determine the temperature or to regulate it, so a reasonably standardized procedure would be to keep the fire going briskly for four hours, then allow it to die of its own accord. The clay objects may be removed the following day.

Tools

Tools for modeling clay are made of wood or metal. You can buy them at any art store, or make them yourself. Good improvised modeling tools are pencils, tongue depressors, and orange sticks. Coat them with Vaseline to prevent sticking.

Do your modeling on a wooden plank. Clay has natural oils in it, and manufactured clays often have oils introduced during preparation, to keep them soft and pliant. This will stain any good table top, so protect your working surface with newspapers.

Some Simple Claycraft Techniques

Slab modeling in clay is a professional pottery method which is so simple that the ordinary youngster can understand the steps involved. The procedure is used to make anything from ash trays, figurines, and paperweights to serious sculpture.

Any self-hardening type of clay (a clay not having an oil base) can

1   2

Simple claycraft technique demonstrated by Eleanor Ackman. 1. Clay is rolled into pancake slab with rolling pin. 2. A knife then traces along edges of cardboard cutouts, slicing into clay and duplicating the form of a fish. 3. Clay is next shaped and joined to other segments over a hump of plaster or clay of appropriate shape. The segments are

be used with the slab method. Let us assume the use of ordinary moist clay, the variety sold at art stores everywhere, coming in several different colors.

ROLLING THE CLAY

When you are ready to begin a project, add water to the clay to make a thick dough. Knead this with the fingers, then wedge it to remove air bubbles. This consists of tearing the clay to pieces and squeezing it together again. Roll out the clay with a rolling pin on a wooden board which has been covered with a piece of damp cloth. The thickness of the slab is determined by placing two wood blocks or yardsticks of the desired depth on each side of the clay slab. The rolling pin rides along the sticks and thus will not go deeper than this track. Here are a few suggested depths for rolling slabs:

removed after shaping, joined together. 4. Once fairly dry, fish can be decorated (incised) with a pointed tool such as orange stick coated with Vaseline, nutpick, pencil, wooden toothpick, or a regular modeling tool. When dry, fish can be painted or left in natural color. (*Photos:* Des Moines Register and Tribune)

Decorative tiles	⅜	inch
Jewel box	⅜	”
Book-end tiles	¾	”
Candy dish and cigarette box	⅜	”
Animal forms	¼	”
Holiday favors and tree ornaments	¼	”

CUTTING OUT THE CLAY SHAPE

The base for a free form, like candy dishes and small containers, may be cut out and trimmed directly from the rolled slab of clay. A straight-edged ruler and pocketknife are adequate for the job. For intricate shapes, you will do better by first making a cardboard pattern in the desired shape. Place the cardboard over the clay slab and slice along the edges.

It is important to weld the sides and bottom carefully together during assembly of the slabs. The sides are made by slicing strips of clay to the desired depth, then standing these on the base piece. Always keep the clay moist while working on it. Every few minutes, wrap a damp cloth over the work and allow it to stand for perhaps ten seconds. It is good practice to roughen the bottom of two pieces where they will join together, using any handy tool. This creates a degree of dovetailing which imparts strength. To further strengthen the weld, roll small balls of clay in your palms, flatten them into long, cigarlike coils and wedge these into the joining point. It is the tightness of the weld which gives the piece strength.

Shaped or modeled clay which breaks during the modeling may be easily mended by introducing to the body a solution of sodium silicate, commonly known as water glass. (This is also useful for cementing cardboard bases to clay objects.)

FINISHING YOUR CLAY PIECE

Before clay shapes are set aside to dry, they may be decorated with relief or incised designs. To do this, press a pointed tool into the clay, cutting in a design to the desired depth. Do not cut too deeply; a heavy scratch is sufficient. If the surface of the clay is to be perfectly smooth, sponge it with a rag or wet fingers, applying enough pressure to eliminate any nicks and to round the edges. Interesting textures can be achieved on the surface by pressing rough burlap, pieces of bamboo, coins, or other textured objects into the clay. A rasp and a comb also impart regular designs.

DRYING THE OBJECT

Slow drying prevents warping and cracking and is necessary even when an object is to be fired. Cover the work with a damp cloth for a couple of days before exposing it to air for the final drying. Turn the work at intervals to insure even drying. The room should not be hot; normal temperature is best.

THE PLASTER HUMP METHOD

In addition to the free-formed slab technique, you may wish to try the hump method, which uses any other hollow object as a form of mold. Either a plaster cast (the hump) is first made from the object, or the object is used directly as a mold for the clay. A hump can be made in an ordinary bowl or piece of crockery that is relatively shallow and has a smooth interior. The final clay piece will then duplicate this interior. First, the inside of the bowl is thoroughly greased with Vaseline, so that the plaster will release easily when it hardens. A liquid solution of plaster of Paris is poured into the mold to the depth desired for the hump. When the plaster sets, it is removed and sanded to get rid of the Vaseline.

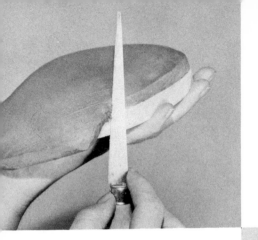

Plaster hump method consists of pressing a slab of moist clay over a plaster of Paris form, then trimming away excess. *(Photos: Illustragraph)*

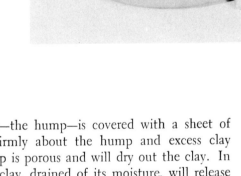

When plaster has absorbed water from clay, the clay will release itself from the hump. It is then sponged, dried, and decorated with paints or incising tool.

Finally, your new shaping piece—the hump—is covered with a sheet of slabbed clay. This is pressed firmly about the hump and excess clay trimmed away. The plaster hump is porous and will dry out the clay. In about an hour, the leather-hard clay, drained of its moisture, will release itself from the plaster. Pick it off and set it down to complete its final drying.

The other hump method consists of using a bowl for the hump. Place a ⅜-inch-thick slab of clay in the bowl and press it down tightly after first coating the interior of the bowl with Vaseline or lard. The clay will eventually dry enough to release itself. This is a slow process, however.

Freehand clay objects thus created are reasonably permanent even without firing. Once fired in a kiln, they will be adaptable for colored glazing and will endure for centuries.

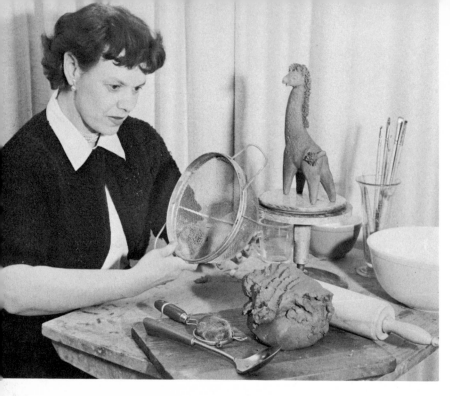

Everyday kitchen tools make excellent modeling equipment. Thelma Frazier Winter uses everything from a breadboard to a sieve. *(Photo: Robert Hoffner)*

Ceramic Sculpture Tips

Using inexpensive kitchen tools like a rolling pin, potato scraper, and wire sieve, artist Thelma Winter turns out striking ceramic figurines much as any housewife produces tempting cookies. They sell for excellent prices, for each is a hand-crafted little masterwork. Here are a few of her budget-minded tricks.

The refrigerator is a handy place to store clay, keeping it soft and moist. And the oven of a kitchen stove will hasten the drying out of finished ceramics, preparatory to permanent firing in a kiln. Do not turn the stove temperature up; just the heat of the pilot light is sufficient.

For those interested in making their hobby pay its way, Thelma Winter's technique is a logical one: work and think in large numbers. It's just as easy to make up a large batch of ceramics at one time as it is to do them one by one. A plaster of Paris mold proves sensible when you are turning out many copies of the first ceramic piece. Just squeeze in the clay, clap the two halves of the mold together, take them apart, and remove the copy. Slight variations can be achieved by modeling, if desired, and a high degree of individuality will be achieved during the glazing of the figurines, for each one may be glazed in different hues and color combinations.

A few more kitchen-inspired tricks, handy for animal sculpture: the clay can be rolled on a pastry board or any wooden plank. A twisted coat hanger makes a good armature on which you may build up your clay. Fine hair is simulated by squeezing clay through a kitchen sieve; longer hair comes out through a larger sieve or strainer. The fur or feathers of bunnies, birds, and chickens are modeled with a potato scraper. Look around your kitchen—you'll find plenty of handy tools for similar purposes.

This rooster (20 inches high) and hen (16 inches high) were directly built by the clay method. They are glazed in brilliant blue-green borax glaze. Unglazed surfaces were treated with black engobe. Firing was done in a kiln. (*Courtesy Thelma Frazier Winter*)

Kitchen-Cooked Sculpture

A new modeling material is on the market which dries to rock hardness after just fifteen minutes' baking in an ordinary kitchen oven! This low-cost vinylite plastic material is called Pyrocon and should prove a boon for those on small budgets.

Use it just as you would any ordinary modeling clay. It is pliant, nonsticky enough for children to handle without muss or mishap. If not baked, it can be used over and over again. Cooked in a stove at moderate heat, the modeled objects become permanent works of art.

Pyrocon comes in many brilliant colors, including red, yellow, blue, green, terra cotta, black, and white. Other hues can be created by intermixing these colors and kneading them together. The pliable substance

More of Thelma Frazier Winter's ceramics. The figures from "Alice in Wonderland" are, of course, the Queen and Jack of Hearts, and the White Rabbit. They are made of terra cotta and painted white, red, and black. They stand approximately eight inches high. (*Photo: Cleveland Museum of Art*)

The new Pyrocon plastigel modeling material may be worked by hand or with any ordinary modeling tool. It comes in bright colors, stays pliant without moistening, and can then be baked to finished hardness in the kitchen oven.

lends itself readily to shaping and mottling with sculpture tools or an orange stick. The white variety can even be fired, then colored with crayons or poster paints.

One special feature of Pyrocon's use is its ability to remain soft for long intervals without moistening.

A number of sculptural ideas rendered in Pyrocon are illustrated in this chapter. Any surface to which the material will adhere and which will stand a temperature of 350° F. for a quarter hour can serve as the building armature. Because Pyrocon protects a fragile base and adds its own strength to the construction, such delicate forms as a sculptured rose are possible without fear of the parts' breaking to pieces during heating.

When modeling, work on a flat tabletop or a breadboard. A bit of talcum powder dusted over your hands will prevent the material from sticking while you are kneading it. If Pyrocon becomes too pliable, place it in a refrigerator for a few minutes and it will return to the proper hardness for modeling.

The material does not shrink during firing. It takes perfect impressions from molds and you can create your own original molds out of it, bake these, and use them as master molds for duplication of the same object.

Some suggested uses for this unusual modeling medium: for making animal forms, puppet heads, dolls, paperweights, toys, and novelty favors.

Pyrocon comes in pint or quart packages, or by the case for school use. Developed by the Bakelite Company, it may be obtained through Transogram Company, 200 Fifth Avenue, New York 10, N. Y.

Roses are carved of Pyrocon, mounted as earrings, and baked in a kitchen oven for permanent hardness.

Sketches show how Thelma Frazier Winter's terra-cotta figure, "Persephone," was worked out. Arrows indicate free flow of air to speed hardening process. Clay bridges, such as the hair, give support where needed.

Tile Decorating

Uses for decorative tiles are manifold today. You can place them in your kitchen, face a fireplace or border a playroom wall, adapt them for drink coasters, make party favors and place cards, and spruce up your mailbox or address plate through this claycraft technique.

Tiles come in various sizes, usually 4 by 4, or 6 by 6 inches, and cost only a few cents each. These are either in bisque (unfired) or glazed in various colors. Bisque is colored with ceramic glazes by the craftsman; pre-glazed tileware can also be overglazed or merely decorated with oil paints. One advantage of using bisque tile is that you can adapt it to sgraffito (scratched) decorating, incising, carving, and to slip decorating, a technique in which more liquid-like clay is added to make a raised design.

The selection of a decorative motif is determined by the use to which the tile will be put. For kitchens, the motif might be nature forms, sea shells, stylized abstractions, representations of various foods, or herbs and flower shapes. For a den or playroom you might try sophisticated abstractions, jinglets, silhouettes and mottoes. For the nursery, songs and rhymes are obvious themes, as are stuffed animals, storks, and fairy tales.

Tiles intended for table use should be backed with felt or have cork "feet" to keep them from scratching the table surface. You can hang tiles on walls by gluing a package tag on back and punching a hole near the top. A looseleaf reinforcing circle is then gummed over the hole to prevent tearing and the tile can be hung from a small nail.

Tiles are easy to keep clean; a wipe of a damp cloth does the job.

Hand-decorated tiles by Ralf.

Plain white plates painted with oil colors by students at State Teachers College, Kutztown, Pennsylvania.

Let us suppose you want to start from scratch, painting on a single preglazed tile, purchased at a builder's supply store. The procedure:

First, clean your tile with soap and water and dry it. Then apply a coat of turpentine. This makes the surface tacky enough to accept pencil lines. Now, draw or trace on your motif, then color it with Dek-All or any similar oil-base colors, applied with a water-color brush. (If a mistake is made, wipe it away with a clean cloth and start again.) Once the design is completed, put the tile in your kitchen oven for a half hour, at 350° F. Then set it aside to cool and air-dry. When it has dried, wash the tile in soap and water to remove dirt, pencil marks, and turpentine residue. The same general procedure is employed when working with bisque tileware, except that the tile is cleaned only with a damp rag and you do your painting with china painting glazes.

For large projects, purchase tiles in money-saving carton lots. The number of tiles in a carton will depend on their size. The 6-by-6 type comes 90 to a carton; the 6-by-4½ size packs 126 to a carton, and 4-by-4 tiles will usually be 180 to the carton. It is also possible to obtain circular tiles and those in elliptical shapes. These are ordered in quantity from manufacturers. The best address source is the Manhattan telephone directory or the classified section of any large city phone book. Usually, tile makers will grant discounts only on fairly large orders—no less than two cartons.

Using Ceramic Colors

Ceramic colors are specifically manufactured for decorating pottery, china, and tiles. These are applied to a glazed tile, then fired.

What is ceramic color? Is it water color or oil color? Ceramic color is a medium all its own. Both oil and water color would vanish from the surface of a piece of work fired in the relatively high heats of a ceramic kiln.

Ceramic colors are basically mineral (that is, metal) oxides. In their true form they appear gray-to-black. The final color is imparted by the action of high heat, which fuses the oxide, creating a beautiful green or blue, a brilliant red or orange. The color possibilities are almost endless. Each mineral creates a specific color when fired at a specific temperature. However, in order to apply any ceramic paint, a medium must be utilized. This is usually water or oil.

To avoid confusion, manufacturers add a bit of harmless coloring, but this actually is burned up once the piece is in the kiln. It is added chiefly for rapid identification and to make the painting of colors easier.

The colors are fired at kiln temperatures which may run upwards of 2000° F., depending on the glaze selected. Ceramic glazing is a science, and each color requires a specific temperature to reach its ultimate hue. Full information on this is available at ceramic supply stores and we will not go into detail here. For the average decorator, using oil colors on glazed white tiles will provide entirely satisfactory results. And when oil-base Dek-All is used, the firing for permanency is simply a matter of baking the tile in a kitchen oven at 350° for a half-hour.

9

Carved wood pigeon (Colonial Williamsburg).

Carving Wood,
Leather, and Plastics

Working on Wood

AN OBVIOUS REASON for the popularity of carving is the simplicity of the initial equipment—a piece of wood and a sharp knife. As the enthusiast progresses, he may wish to refine his work with sandpaper, some staining, possibly a coat of paint. It is not until the basic skill has been mastered that the average wood sculptor need concern himself with precision tools. When that day finally arrives, he can purchase, for a few dollars, a compact woodworking kit.

Every woodworking shop should have a good array of these tools. Complete assortments are sold in portable chests at varying prices. Good tools, properly cared for, will last a lifetime.

SELECTING THE WOOD

Soft, clear-grained wood is best. White pine and sugar pine are inexpensive and popular choices. Other excellent woods are cedar (for grained effect) and willow (for a gray finish). Avoid the harder woods—mahogany, maple, walnut, birch. They require greater skill. For the youngest carvers, a hard grade of balsa is best, requiring little pressure to cut its surface.

[89]

Below: An ideal carving tool is this form of X-acto knife. It prevents razor edges from slipping and provides a firm grip.

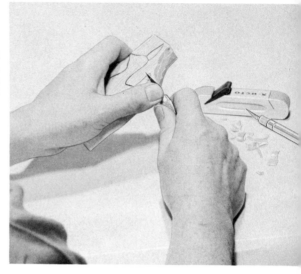

Carving is done on a block of soft wood traced with the design. Strokes follow the grain. The finished sanded and painted figure is shown opposite.

In choosing a block of wood, be certain it is free of cracks and large knots. Kiln-dried wood is superior, for wood so processed is not liable to internal cracking, called "checking." Carve in the direction of the grain; cutting across grain encourages splitting of thin parts.

CUTTING TECHNIQUE IN WOOD CARVING

There are two basic methods: pushing or pulling the knife across the material. The knife must always be sharp, so keep an eye on your fingers when pulling the blade. A dull knife is more dangerous than a sharp one; it is more apt to stick or jerk. Experienced craftsmen prefer heavy knives with sharp blades which can be inserted quickly and removed when dull. A knife such as that manufactured by X-acto Company is ideal.

PROCEDURE IN CARVING

The first step in a project is to create a pattern on tracing paper and then trace this onto the carving material. Trace it in its various dimen-

sions: top, bottom, sides. Use a hard pencil for the purpose. For soft woods, you can whittle with your knife; for harder woods you may need to do the heavy work with a band saw, jig saw, or coping saw. The finer details are invariably achieved with knife and sandpaper.

Finishing

The whittled object can be finished with stain, or polished with fine sandpaper and left in its natural state. For durability, a coat of clear shellac is recommended. This will also make cleaning a simple matter. A high gloss is imparted by rubbing the wood with sandpaper, then either waxing it with floor polish or painting it with enameled oil paint. If you are applying paint, first seal the wood's pores with an impregnation of shellac and denatured alcohol, in fifty-fifty solution. After painting, sand it lightly, apply another coat of paint, then give it a brisk rubbing with floor wax. The same general procedure is followed for high glossing a stained carving.

Carving on Leather

Craftsman's leather comes in a wide selection of materials. *Alligator* is popular for making billfolds, but it cannot be tooled. These skins range in size up to 14 inches wide by 60 inches in length. *Calfskin* is excellent for billfolds and handbags, and it can be tooled. The skins measure up to 14 square feet. *Cowhide*, for belts and hard-wearing accessories, can be tooled, carved, and stamped too. Skin size: up to 25 square feet. *Lambskin* is used for linings, purses, and belts and comes in the form of suede, or in many different embossed grains. The skin size: up to 9 square feet. *Lizard*, for purses and billfolds, comes in almost any color, but cannot be tooled. The skins are small, about 9 inches by 17 inches at most. *Morocco* is a goat skin that measures up to 14 square feet or so, and is popular for making book bindings, billfolds, belts, linings, purses, and similar items. *Pigskin* is good for letter cases, small sewing boxes, sewed gloves, and billfolds. It can be tooled, but this requires an expert. Pigskins range in size up to 20 square feet. *Ostrich* is an expensive material that comes in russet, brown, or black and is beautiful for book covers and top-quality billfolds. The skins go to about 14 square feet in size. *Sheepskin* comes in many forms of suede. While it cannot be tooled quite as well as calfskin, it is less expensive. It lends itself to the making of purses, linings, book covers, bookmarks, etc. Skin size: to 9 square feet. *Steerhide* is the best tooling leather, except for the costly calfskin. It may be used for almost any type of carving project. It comes in natural or two-tone colors, and is of varying weights. The hides measure up to 28 square feet.

DYES AND STAINS FOR LEATHERWORK

Manufacturers color leather with wood or coal tar dyes. There are also other dyes available to the craftsman at most shops: *Water dye* (aniline dye) is a powder that is mixed with hot water. The leather is immersed in this bath, or the dye can be brushed on. For a softer effect use an *oil stain*. This is thinned with turpentine, then applied to the leather with a brush and immediately wiped off. For elementary craftsmen and youngsters, the cheapest and most satisfactory dye is *spirit dye*. This is a powder. A good *waterproof ink*, like those made by Higgins or Pelikan, is also a relatively inexpensive dye. The inks come in many colors and are handy for dyeing the edges of leather goods and for drawing small designs onto their surface.

TOOLS AND EQUIPMENT

Tools should last a lifetime. Buy quality tools; they are not very expensive. Among the most commonly called for are: *Skiving knife*, for cutting out leather patterns from the skins. *Awl*, used to spread open thong slits for the insertion of laces. (A nut pick makes a handy substitute for this tool.) *Revolving punch*, to punch through the leather with its six rotating "teeth" of various sizes. Select the one which your work requires and spin the head to the proper tooth. *Drive punch*, used for making round holes in places which the revolving punch cannot reach. The *thonging chisel* makes thong slits. It resembles a flat table fork in appearance. A tool known as the *tracer* does just what its name implies; traces designs onto the leather. Handy for repeat patterns. If the job of tracing is not too fine, you can substitute a screwdriver or a mimeograph stylus for this purpose. The point of such instruments must be thin, however. The *ball tool* is used for stippling and embossing a design onto leather. One of the most commonly used tools of all is the common *mallet*, a hard wood hammer that is banged onto the thonging chisel or similar tool to drive it through the leather surface. Another good piece of equipment is the *embossing wheel*. It looks like the revolving head of a bulldozer and its small wheels are studded with blunt points which roll a border along the leather. The embossing heads come in several sizes, for different purposes. The *modeler* tool is used to do two jobs. It has two ends, the small one being intended as a design tracer, and the larger one for putting down backgrounds or embossing. It looks like a dentist's pick. A *steel square*, or "*L*" *square*, serves for laying out and cutting straight lines in the leather.

All these tools are basic, though only a few will be necessary for any single project. It is worth while to have them handy.

Leather cutting procedure

Select a design and cut drawing paper to the exact size of the item. If the object is to have folds or creases, duplicate this with your paper dummy. Determine the placement and space allowance for such things as buttons, lacings along edges, etc. Then trace the design onto the leather with carbon paper. You will find it a timesaver to fashion templates—that is, temporary guides or patterns of paper, cardboard, or even thin metal—which help you in cutting out the shapes and otherwise guide you in repeating the pattern. When several copies of a design are to be made, make the templates of tin, cut with shears. They can be used indefinitely.

The cutting is done with a sharp knife. Put the leather onto a *soft* pine board for this purpose. Soft pine is preferred in this case as it has no raised grain to deflect the knife blade. Place your steel square over the hide and cut out the rectangular piece of leather containing your traced design. Hold the knife blade at a 45° angle and slice through the skin with one stroke. Then lay your template over the leather piece and cut around it with the knife. The leather is now ready for tooling.

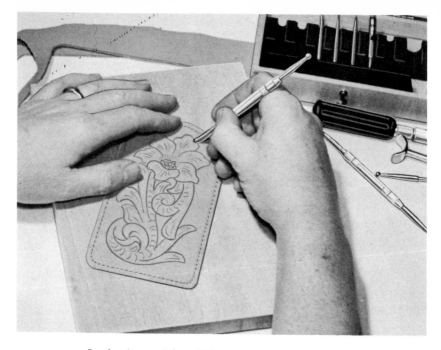

Leather is carved from hide and then tooled in a surface design. Among the most popular projects are the making of billfolds, belts, key wallets, bookmarks, and purses. Leather skins are available in many varieties and the hides are purchased either full size or in precut sizes.

TOOLING

Leather must be moistened before you go to work on it with your tools. Sponge on water to the flesh side of the skin, using a patting motion. When the back side darkens, the skin is sufficiently moist. Moisten the entire skin, not just the work area. This insures even drying and uniformity of color. The skin should not ooze water when you cut it. Dry to damp consistency on a hard, flat surface like marble or glass, for leather will take the shape of the surface.

The design is now traced onto the leather. Tape your tracing paper in position and, using a hard pencil or stylus, lightly press down the motif. Pick up one corner of the paper frequently and inspect the progress of your tracing. Impart just enough pressure to mark down guide lines of the design that you will later tool.

Once the design is traced, you can start tooling the leather. Simple outline tooling is a good introductory method. This consists of merely pressing down the motif's outlines with a blunt tracing point. The next technique to try might be flat modeling. It is similar to outlining, but larger areas are depressed within the outlined motif. For this use a broad

Finished hand-tooled key-wallet design with lace-stitched edging. Leather can be finished with stains (as here) or with inks and dyes, or it can be left in its natural color.

or medium modeler tool. Try the technique when making monograms. Work carefully and avoid scraping your fingernails on the damp leather. Remember: damping is done on the reverse side of the leather (the rough skin side). Outlining is done on the smoother surface. Keep adding water as required to maintain a moderate dampness. All modeling is done by holding the tool as you would a pencil.

If you wish to raise a design, turn the leather over and press up the motif with a ball tool. As the design is raised, turn the work face up again and re-outline around the raised portions. To hold the raised details you will have to force a mixture of cotton wool and paste into the recessed portions in the back side with your ball tool. This will dry firmly and may be further reinforced by adding a liner behind the leather afterward.

You may further mark the leather with stamping tools which actually punch a preconceived motif into the surface. The die tool is struck with a mallet and the motif is thus sunk into the leather. You may use this same method to stamp or punch designs of your own innovation, using appropriately shaped metal tools. If you use a sharp knife to cut designs, this is called incising.

[95]

Carving Plastics

Perhaps you will want to try your hand at carving in one of the new synthetic mediums known as plastics. Softer types can be whittled easily. First, experiment on pieces of wood until you can handle your knife competently; then you are ready to carve plastics. Your earliest work should be on the soft plastic material commonly known as cellulose acetate. It comes in blocks, expressly for carving purposes. An advantage of plastics is the absence of grain, and the many beautiful colors in which the material comes. The cost is quite moderate, often less than wood.

Plastic can be cut with a sharp knife. Among the Christmas-tree ornaments here are hearts and stars cut from a thin sheet of plastic and decorated with Dek-All paint. Metallic cords tie through holes drilled in upper section of cutouts.

10

Woodcut by Eric Gill.

Block Printing

Linoleum

YOU START WITH a block of wood that has been covered with a piece of gray-toned linoleum. You end with a piece of handcrafted printing that can have boldness, crudity, or delicacy of line.

Linoleum is often preferred to wood for carving because it is more easily incised. The results are basically the same. Two renderings are possible: negative and positive delineation. In the former, the black areas predominate, with the art shown mostly as white "blanks," like a blackboard drawing. The reverse is true in positive work. The amount of work involved depends upon the area to be gouged away with your cutting tool. Whatever is chiseled away will not print—thus it comes out as white space.

Special, thick printing inks are used. They are available at most art stores. Your other materials consist of a pencil or piece of charcoal, cutting tools (which come in a set of six gouge points for about a dollar, plus another dollar or so for the handle into which they are interchangeably inserted), a brayer (roller), piece of plate glass, and the paper, fabric, or other material upon which you will print. Instead of using the regulation tools, you may substitute a penknife, razor blade, awl, scalpel, or any similar gouge. Turpentine or benzine is needed for cleaning up.

The first step is to draw or trace your design on the linoleum surface. Because the design or lettering on the block will be reversed in printing,

Tools and materials for linoleum-block printing consist of blocks, pencil for tracing design onto block, linoleum cutting blades and handle, and rubber brayer for spreading ink over carved surface. *(Photo: Daniel Firestone)*

don't forget to draw it in reverse on the block. Then begin carving. It is wise to carve sparingly rather than too much at a time. You can remove more from the block, but you cannot replace cut areas. At any desired time you can stop working, roll some ink over the block, and make a proof. Proofing consists of squeezing ink on the glass, rolling it with the brayer, then rolling the tool over the carved block. The wet block is positioned over a sheet of paper which lies atop several thicknesses of soft blotter, then it is hammered with a mallet or your fist or stepped on to stamp down the design. Examine your proof carefully. Make corrections as necessary. When the block has been carved to your satisfaction, you as necessary. When the block has been carved, you can print on paper or any flat surface that will take the ink.

MAKING YOUR OWN PRINTING INK

Although quality block printing ink costs only about fifty cents a tube, those readers who wish to make their own can try the following recipe:

    1 part boiled linseed oil
    1 part varnish
    2 parts powder tempera

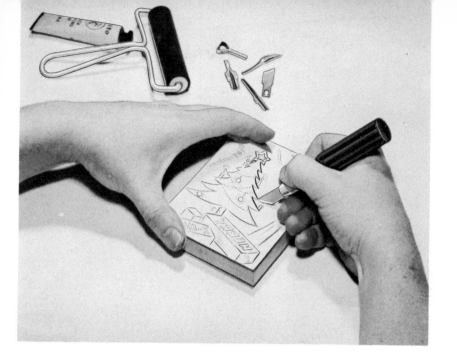

Carving on a linoleum printing block.

Add a few drops of linseed oil to the tempera and mix until it is the consistency of thick paste. Now slowly add the remainder of the linseed oil and then pour in the varnish and stir well. The resulting medium should be a moderate paste that can be placed on a plate of glass and rolled with a rubber brayer to form a thin smear of color across the glass. Load your brayer by rolling it from several directions, then transfer this to the surface of the carved linoleum block.

Printing methods

The most popular way to print is by rolling ink on the block, then laying it face down over the blank paper on which it is to print. Press down firmly, pound it lightly with your balled fist, or tap it with a hammer.

An alternate method is to place the coated linoleum block face up and lightly position your paper on top. Then run a rolling pin, the bowl of a spoon, or a spatula across the top several times to transfer the motif.

For long pieces of paper or yard goods you may remove the linoleum from its wood block (or simply do your carving on thin linoleum sheeting), place it printing side down on the printing material, and then run both pieces through a clothes wringer.

Set of linoleum carving tools by X-acto offers wide
variety of gouging points. They make finished work
professional in appearance by imparting broad and fine
lines, straight cuts, and curves.

Multiple repeat design is shown on carved linoleum
block. Reproduction can be in one color, or, if additional color is desired, one or more design elements
can be eliminated and cut into a second and third
block.

"Nativity." Linoleum block print by Carmen Macia.

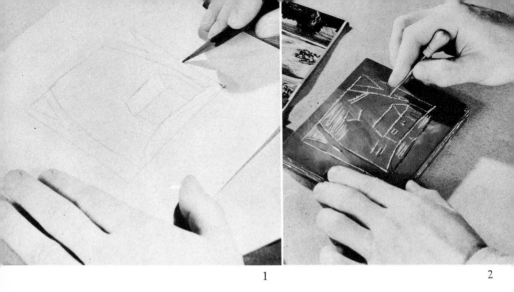

1

2

1. First step in preparing a linoleum block is to sketch motif actual size, then trace this onto linoleum surface. 2. Design is cut deeply with a cutting tool. Depressed areas will not print, uncut portions will come out as solid color. 3. After motif is cut, ink is rolled across surface with rubber brayer. Rolling is done from several directions to

A block print can be done in several colors. Carve a different block for each color, then print each in its proper position when the previous color has dried. Place a ruler along the edge of the printing paper and carefully mark the position for each color area before actually printing. Although you can print one color over another, the results are not predictable. The ink is thick and not very translucent. Once dried, it seldom shows through the next layer enough to produce the combined hues you may be seeking.

When printing on fabric, always tack it down smoothly before you begin.

Among the printing possibilities are bookplates; Christmas cards; framed prints for wall hanging; decorated scarves, blouses, handkerchiefs, ties; table linens; wide leather belts; book ends; programs and handbills; letterheads.

Block Printing with an Eraser

You can use an artgum eraser and a rubber stamp pad to produce inexpensive block prints. It's a simple project which young people will enjoy and which advanced craftsmen occasionally use for making test designs prior to the more painstaking carving in creating linoleum or wood block prints.

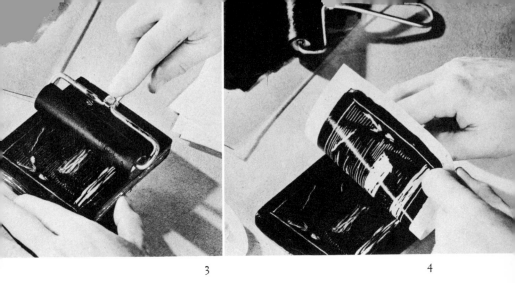

3   4

insure full coverage. 4. Place paper, fabric, or other printing surface against inked block and apply pressure to transfer design. Use fist or a rubber mallet over protected surface to apply pressure, or simply stand on the block. *(Courtesy Bassons Industries Corporation)*

Your equipment consists of a ten-cent artgum eraser, razor blade, soft drawing pencil, and stamp pad.

The motif is roughed out on paper with your soft lead pencil (in reverse if necessary); then the back of the paper is rubbed thoroughly with the pencil to make a tracing paper of it. The design is now retraced with the paper placed on top of the eraser. A hard pencil or mimeograph stylus is a handy tool for this purpose. When the paper is lifted, the design has been transferred onto the artgum and is ready for carving.

A single-edged razor blade now is pressed along the design outline, cutting to a depth of about a quarter inch. Work carefully and remember that the eraser is very soft and will crumble easily. It is better to dig away too little than too much; you can test print at any point to see how well the motif has been carved away. When the design has been cut out, press the eraser firmly onto a rubber-stamp pad and cover the raised areas with the ink. Then use this block as you would normally use a rubber stamp. The motif may be stamped in any color onto a sheet of paper or fabric. If additional colors are desired, carve separate erasers for each color and carefully place the artgum in position before printing it.

This project will save you time and money in testing simple designs. Obviously, it cannot be employed for intricate carving because of the softness of the material.

Since the "block" measures less than two inches in length and only an inch or so in width, the motif should be one intended for repeats—as in making border designs. It is an interesting introduction to block printing and one which affords the artist experience in carving, planning designs, and learning to work with simple boldness.

AND TRY USING A POTATO

The same general procedure is followed in using a raw potato as a printing block. To do this, cut a large potato in half and carve its surface with your sharp blade. Bear in mind that the areas which are cut away will fall below the printing surface and thus print blank, while the remaining, uncarved areas will do the actual printing. For fine lines or dots use an awl or mimeograph stylus to punch down the printing surface. Both the artgum and potato, particularly the latter, have a fugitive lifespan, but because of their negligible cost they may be discarded and new printing blocks carved after a hundred or so applications.

Simple designs made with carved gum eraser (*left*) and a carved potato (*right*). Second colors were added with additional stamps and highlights were painted freehand.

Textile Decorating

Silk Screening

THE SILK-SCREEN printing process originated in China some two thousand years ago.

By this method, posters, program covers, and cards may be printed in quantity and in a number of colors at a surprisingly low cost. It is the only practical technique by which printing may be done successfully on glass, wood, and other objects which cannot be run through a press. Many textiles and wallpapers are printed by the silk-screen method.

The equipment may be built easily, or purchased for a very small sum. A list of the necessary equipment includes the stencil, stencil knife, a frame over which has been stretched an open-mesh silk, adhering liquid, a rubber squeegee, turpentine, removing liquid, printing ink, amber lacquer, tape, tacks, newspaper, and rags.

The frame is usually constructed of 1-inch by 2-inch lumber to a standard poster size. It is advisable to allow 1 inch to each side of the screen's inside measurements, for freedom of flowing the ink over the stencil. Over the frame a piece of silk bolting cloth or organdy (which is not so durable as bolting cloth) must be tightly stretched and made secure, first with tacks, and then with shellac. Care is used in shellacking the edges so that none of the shellac covers the printable portion of the silk. The screen is then hinged to a plywood board slightly larger than the frame. When this is done, it is ready to receive the stencil.

THE FIRST STEP IS DESIGNING

The motif is planned as a color sketch, exact size, and this is taped onto the work board or drawing table. Then the transparent stencil, made of a special thick paper (and available in most art shops), is taped on top of this guide, and the areas which are to print are cut out with a stencil knife. Only the lacquered layer is cut. The remaining areas will act as a mask, holding back the printing color. Most craftsmen prefer to draw these printing areas directly on the stencil with a hard pencil, tracing only those portions which are pertinent to the specific color which that stencil will print. A separate stencil is made for each subsequent color printing. Each stencil should be cross-marked in each of its corners so that registering will be exact and simple to achieve.

ADHERING THE STENCIL TO THE SCREEN

Commercial adhesive is used to fasten the stencil on the screen for printing. The stencil is taped beneath the screen so that the lacquered side of the stencil is against the screen. Then newspapers are spread beneath the frame to protect the working table and act as a cushion. Now, a soft cloth is soaked with adhering solution and swept across the area of the screen backed by the stencil. Wet a little of the area at a time. A clean dry rag is alternately swept over this to pick up excess liquid as you proceed. This continues until the entire area backed by the stencil has been covered. The stencil will dry in a few minutes, after which the transparent backing of the stencil is zipped off, since it has served its purpose of holding the cut-out elements in place until they have adhered. This backing is discarded. The stencil is now firmly adhered to the screen. Any remaining areas which are not to be printed and which lay outside the border of the stencil are covered with strips of masking tape, or given a coating of amber lacquer. This resists the printing colors and can later be dissolved off, if the screen is to be cleaned for the next stencil. You are now ready to begin printing the first color.

SELECTING PRINTING INKS

Prepared inks in both oil and water color are available for printing on papers or fabrics. The consistency of the printing color is important. Color which is too thin will flow between the stencil and the paper; color which is too thick will not flow through the silk evenly and will not produce an even-textured print.

The material to be printed is placed between the plywood board and the hinged screen. Register marks are made to indicate placement of the printing material on the board. The screen is then lowered and the color is spread over the screen with a rubber squeegee. Plenty of color must be used so that the printing is accomplished with a single stroke. Raise the screen, remove the material, and allow it to dry before attempting to print another color.

The screen is cleaned of water-type inks with water; kerosene or turpentine is used for oil-base inks.

SCREENS ARE REUSABLE

Screens may be used many times by removing the stencil. A special removing liquid is usually sold with the stencil which, when applied to it, has a disintegrating effect, and the particles of the stencil are caught and adhered to a newspaper placed under the screen as a pad.

Designs may be printed in many colors, one after the other, following exactly the same procedure as outlined here, and after the preceding color has been allowed to dry. Interesting effects are obtained by "slipping" a stencil slightly and reprinting it in another color, or through the use of transparent inks. Experience and experimentation will add to the list of effects produced with a silk screen.

SCREENING ON TEXTILES

When textiles are printed by the silk-screen process, it is important to have a suitable working surface. A firm table about three yards in length will enable satisfactory printing of yardage. Cover the table with wall board to make a smooth, even surface. Over this, place newspapers to act as blotters. Many methods are used to score off the table to insure true registration. (One is to mark off the sides in inches and, with the aid of a large T-square, the screen may be moved about, retaining proper position.) The fabric is now pinned firmly to the table.

The oil colors are mixed with a medium that assures the washing of fabrics without loss of color. The dyes are so prepared that they work easily through the screen, and these colors can be dry-cleaned perfectly. Thus, we use *dye* for fabrics that are to be dry-cleaned, and *oil colors* for those to be washed. As the dye is in concentrated form, it is mixed with a basic or clear dye until the right consistency and color value are obtained.

THE PRINTING BEGINS

Place the screen over the fabric at the point where you want the design. Pour a small quantity of dye on the screen at the upper edge. Hold back with a squeegee. (This tool is made of thick ribbon rubber, held in place by a bank of wood that forms a handle.) It is the same width as the working screen. With the aid of the squeegee, pull the dye across the stencil, then lift the screen up carefully again, placing it at the next given point. Pull the dye back over the stencil to the top of the screen. Just enough dye should be placed on the screen at one time to take care of about four motif prints.

Two young silk-screen printers show press on which their display of fabrics were made. (*Courtesy Florida State University*)

Choosing motifs for screen printing

Designs most suitable for silk-screen printing are those that suggest stencil printing or, in other words, print designs. Designs used in weaving should be discouraged for this type of printing. Best of all are picture designs, using a simple motif, repeating and reversing to form an all-over pattern.

Glazed chintz is ideal to work upon. With the addition of metallic powder to the basic dye, amazing effects can be created. Many colors may be printed from the same stencil by blocking or sealing parts of the design and exposing others. Wallpaper printed with the dye gives a glazed design against a dull paper.

Block-print effects can be secured by light and heavy pressure upon the squeegee. Oil-base pigments may be printed through the same screen as described, but different mediums are used to thin and wash paint from the screen.

[108]

Draw-string beach bag made out of a circle of silk-screened fabric in a simple repeat design. *(Courtesy Prang Studios)*

A drawing by an eight-year-old artist, Kathy Schaad, was traced onto a screen and used for an imaginatively decorated tablecloth. *(Courtesy Prang Studios)*

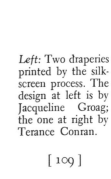

Left: Two draperies printed by the silk-screen process. The design at left is by Jacqueline Groag; the one at right by Terance Conran.

Here is a project to introduce newcomers to the craft. It may be done by children.

For this introductory lesson we will use Genie Handipaint Powder, a product of the Binney and Smith Company. Mix some with water to a stiff consistency. This will be our "ink."

Many variations are possible in the selection of equipment for screening, and in resist methods. With economy in mind, we recommend that beginners use discarded, inexpensive, and available materials. Here are some suggestions.

For Frame: embroidery hoops, cardboard mats, shallow boxes, or old picture frames.

Screening Fabrics: silk, nylon, organdy, curtain scrim, and other mesh fabrics.

Tools: stapler, thumbtacks, mat knife or razor blade, scissors.

For Squeegee: hard rubber window wiper, square caster, pot scraper, cardboard strip, piece of beveled wood molding.

The Printing Medium: Genie Handipaint Powder, mixed with water. Experience alone will determine the exact consistency, since personal choice of value, color, and texture is involved. To Genie, add a little white tempera to mix tints, or gold and silver tempera to provide a metallic color quality. The screen and printing tools wash clean with soap and water.

Paper Materials: gummed tape, to provide measured clean edges on the fabric screen; newspaper, for stencils; white and novelty papers for printing.

Fabrics on Which to Print: any firm fabrics such as heavy cotton, chintz, buckram, Pellon. Place mats, book covers, and other useful printed articles can have a protective coat of shellac.

Resist Materials: original positive and negative stencils, wax coloring crayons, nail polish. (Use turpentine to remove crayon from the screen and acetone to remove nail polish.)

For Extenders: water; glycerin to retard the drying time of the paint and to minimize the clogging of the screen.

For a Baseboard (needed for two or more color registrations). Make it larger than the frame to which it will be hinged, and construct it of plywood or Masonite.

Construction Details. First make the screen by stretching fabric across the underside of a frame. Fasten it securely to all sides of the frame with staples or tacks. It is helpful to have the warp run lengthwise, or follow the warp direction in printing with the squeegee. This insures better registration when extra stencils are used to produce a print of two or more colors.

You may wish to start with a simple stencil of folded paper, which can be cut with scissors, and later progress to other designs cut out with blades or knives. Paper stencils can be adhered to any fabric screen by placing the screen on a moist stencil and pulling the premixed Genie across the top of the screen with a squeegee. Let the applied stencil dry for a moment or two before making more prints.

Wax crayons, applied heavily on an organdy or silk screen, provide a resist method which permits the use of free or deliberate textures as well as line work and small solid areas. Textured materials placed under the organdy and rubbed hard with unwrapped scraps of crayon can start your explorations. Feel free to combine crayon outlines with texture rubbings and with cut paper stencils. If you want opaque areas in the print, hold the organdy to the light to see if the space between the threads is well filled with crayon.

Another resist material which works best on a finely woven screen is nail polish. Apply several coats of polish where opaque areas are desired.

Other Simple Printing Methods. In addition to the types of squeegees listed, try sponges, damp cloths, and even parts of the hand to force the paint through the silk screen.

Multicolor prints, using only one stencil, are obtained by placing several colors of the Genie mixture at one edge of the screen and letting them merge as the squeegee is pulled across the screen. Single color prints can be made on original decorated papers and on commercial novelty papers.

For more variety, place textured materials under white or colored papers before printing on them.

USING PAPER LABELS

Stationery stores carry a wide variety of gummed stickers and label shapes—everything from stars or circles to polka dots and ring binders. If these are glued to the back of a silk-screen stencil paper in repeat motif or scattered, they will make reverse silhouettes during printing. The color prints around the shapes, serving as a background. For example, try white polka dots and stars against a red or blue background. Again, we emphasize that it is not necessary to do freehand designing in order to be a creative artist. The creativity lies in your ability to integrate, plan, and execute the motif.

AQUA TEXTILE COLOR—A RECENT INNOVATION

Every textile decorator and hobbyist will be delighted at the ease with which the newly developed Prang Aqua Textile Colors can be adapted for screen printing. With this ready-to-use medium, you can design and execute beautiful fabric prints—clothing, aprons, table linens, to name just

Stencil is cut on stencil paper with X-acto type knife *(left)*, then fastened to back of silk screen with masking tape. Be sure all non-printing areas, such as at edge of stencil, have been masked out. Paper or fabric is then fastened to table top with tape to prevent slipping, and design is printed by applying color through screen with squeegee *(right)*. Motif can be repeated over as large an area of material as needed by moving screen an inch or two each time.

a few of the creative possibilities—with a minimum of fuss and bother, leaving maximum time for creating.

Children can work with the medium neatly, for cleanup time is literally child's play; just run the screen under tap water, and the residue washes down the drain. Color on tabletops, hands, and clothes vanishes, too, with water washing, yet the colors can be made permanently fast by ironing in the following manner:

When the fabric is dry, place a cloth on top and iron for three minutes at 350° setting (for cottons). Turn the fabric over and repeat the procedure. For heat-sensitive fabrics, iron at 250° per side for five minutes. That's all there is to it!

Aqua Color is used right from the jar, or may be extended by adding water. It is sunfast and lightfast, has no odor. A wide variety of subtle shades are made possible by adding a bit of Toner. While Aqua Color is a natural for screen printing, the same medium may be used for sponge printing.

Sponge Printing

Sponge printing will open up a vast new field for the imaginative decorator. The sponge recommended is the familiar cellulose, synthetic type used for dishwashing. It may be used in a number of ways.

Apron silk-screened
with cock motif.
Alternate rows are
printed later with
second color.

Pouncing with sponges

Squeeze textile color onto a water-dampened sponge and wring it
moderately moist, working the color into it. Then pounce the sponge
against an object (a dry leaf, potato masher, bottle cap, wire mesh, cooky
cutter, paper clips) and press the object, color-side down, onto your
fabric. The design transfers easily and can be used as a repeat motif, or
may be intermixed with other shapes in other colors. Keep a different
sponge for each color.

Sponges for block printing and stencils

Pounce the color-impregnated sponge onto the printing surface of a
wood block or through the open areas of a stencil, then print in usual
manner onto fabric. The wood block, for example (which is simply a piece
of wood onto whose surface a design has been gouged or scratched with a
sharp knife) is "inked" with Aqua Color and neatly laid face down on the
fabric to be decorated. A wooden mallet then is struck over the block,
transferring the design to the material. (You can simply stand on the
block if you have no mallet handy.) In the case of stenciling, the cutout
stencil is positioned over the fabric and the color pounced through the
holes in the paper stencil. This makes a silhouette effect. For more
advanced stencils, silk screening is the answer.

Using sponges as a stamp pad

A large color-impregnated sponge makes an ideal stamp pad. Bits of
oddly shaped rubber, plastics, strings, rubber stamps with stars, or interesting symbols are simply pressed against the sponge and then stamped onto
the fabric.

[113]

Sponge painting. Saturate a clean sponge with Aqua color and use as a stamping pad. Press leaves (or other objects) on sponge, then place colored side down on absorbent paper or a thin fabric. Lay a piece of scrap paper over object chosen and press down firmly so natural design prints as shown at right.

USING SPONGES FOR FREE-SHAPED STAMPS

Tear or scissor pieces of sponge into unusual shapes, then work in Aqua Color and place the torn sponges on your fabric. A light pressure will transfer the design. Experiment with these shapes on scrap material—try light pressure, try heavy pressure (with its slight blurring effect) and even try moving the sponge for abstract color washes.

Using Wax Crayons on Screens

Even the very young can make designs for their clothing and home furnishings! There is a spontaneity about the drawings of a five-year-old which can be captured with Aqua Color, allowing preschoolers to work hand in hand with their parents on a mutual project. Just give them a handful of wax crayons and let them draw directly on E-Z Cut stencil paper, which provides a low-cost, simple screen, and which most art suppliers stock. They can draw in any colors they choose; the wax merely acts as a resist, masking off areas which will print in "white" when the color is squeezed over the art. The color penetrates areas not covered with wax crayon to make a pleasing background. (Afterward, the fabric may be hand-colored for details, or other stencils printed on top for multicolored effects.) The young artist has only two instructions to follow: press hard with the wax crayons and fill in areas solidly. Incidentally, when you are through with the stencil, the excess color can be washed away under water, as usual, and the original crayon drawing framed over a sheet of white paper! It makes a treasured keepsake if protected with glass.

Gummed stickers bought in a stationery store make attractive screen printing motifs. Stick them down on the screen and even up borders with masking tape. Design on blouse (*right*) shows result.

Wax crayon stenciling. Crayon drawing is done with firm hand directly on back of silk screen stretched across embroidery hoop or frame. Aqua textile color is then squeegeed or sponged over wax crayon drawing and prints through areas not covered with crayon. Photo at right shows children's work done by this "resist" method.

Stencil Decorating on Textiles

When we think of stenciling, we are sometimes apt to remember the old-fashioned kind of stencil with ugly broken lines, gaping white spaces left where the designs should have met neatly (usually known as "bridges"). But there is a "new look" in stenciling today. It is easy to achieve and has an appearance both modern and in good taste. No longer is stenciling relegated to making repeat designs on pieces of paper. It is now swiftly and inexpensively adapted to the decoration of fabrics. You can stencil designs of lasting beauty onto clothing, draperies, tablecloths, and napkins, scarves—even coverings for lampshades.

Textile colors are made by a number of manufacturers. They are inexpensive and go a long way. When the painted material is steam-set with a household iron at linen temperature for three minutes, it becomes washfast and sunproof. (Be sure to cover the fabric with a dry cloth while ironing.)

How do you do it? The technique is quite simple. Let's suppose you're going to decorate a tablecloth or draperies. The first step is to make up rough sketches, scaled to the dimension of the material. Try designing simple, bold repeats. Make colored-pencil roughs to visualize the interplay of color and its adaptability into the decorative scheme of your home.

We are now ready to make our stencil. A black outline drawing of the original idea is sketched on regular sketching paper by working actual size. Next, color it with paint or wax crayon. It is this drawing which will serve as the guide from which you will make your stencils. Each choice of color used will require a separate stencil.

The stencils are cut out of regular wax-paper stencil stock, obtainable at any art supplier. This stock is transparent and thus makes cutting of the design onto its surface a simple matter. Once the design is satisfactory from the standpoint of balance and coloring, fasten your stencil on top of the drawing with masking tape and trace the design with a lead pencil. Trace only those sections which are to be printed in the same color. In each subsequent stencil tracing, you will indicate the other colors involved—one stencil for each color. When the tracing is completed, examine it again for possible errors or last-minute changes. Is it all right? Then go over the pencil tracing with pen and ink for greater legibility.

Now cut out the stencil with a knife or razor blade. Do your cutting over heavy cardboard. Remember the principle involved—whatever areas you cut out and remove from the stencil will print, and those areas *not* cut out will block the paint. Repeat this procedure for each stencil.

Once all the stencils are cut, you are ready to start printing.

Place a large blotter on the tabletop. Rule two bold black lines at one corner, at right angles to each other. This will provide a corner into which each stencil can be positioned for proper register. Place your fabric on

1

2

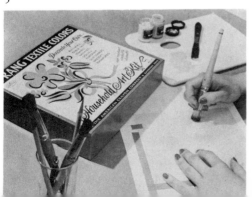

3
4

Stenciling on fabric. 1. Trace design on tracing paper, making right-angle guide line on left corner, at least 2 inches from design. 2. Trace design (and guide line) on stencil paper with hard pencil. Go over lines with pen and ink. 3. Cut motifs in stencil (place cardboard underneath). Keep checking original for areas to cut out. Also make stencil for second color. 4. De-sized fabric is placed on white blotter. Note guide line and masking tape which shows where stencil will fit. 5. Place stencil in position, fasten with drafting tape, and start brushing color off stencil toward inside of material. 6. After design is colored, let dry, then apply second stencil for second color. Let dry for twenty-four hours; then place damp cloth over work and iron to set color. The table mat and napkin are stenciled with the same design.

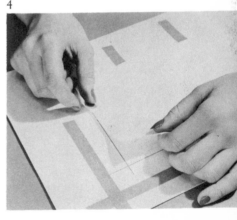

5

6

the blotter, with one corner squaring up in the ruled right angle. Once it lines up correctly, affix it with masking tape.

It is now necessary to line up the stencil. Make another right angle with masking tape, about two inches outside the two edges of the fabric. This will be the guide for all stencils used. Place your first stencil in the masking-tape corner and fasten it securely with more bits of masking tape. The holes in, the stencil are now over the fabric. The printing begins.

Use a stiff bristle brush to pounce on the color. Your paint, which comes from the bottle unmixed, should be diluted with textile-color extender in any ratio that creates the desired shade. Dip the brush into the paint and begin to paint through the stencil. The best methods for application are stippling, rotating, pouncing, or cross-hatching. Work smoothly.

Allow the paint to set a minute or so before lifting the stencil. You should now have completed the first color application. The same procedure is followed for each subsequent color. These steps are shown·on page 117 in sequence photographs.

PAPER DOILY AND RUBBER CEMENT DESIGNS

Here's a project developed by art teacher Dorothy Harkins. To try it, buy yourself a box of paper doilies at the local five-and-ten-cent store. Select a good brush, some water-soluble textile paints, a printing pad, and a bottle of rubber cement, and you're ready to try another unusual experiment in decorating fabrics with screens and stencils. The paper doilies are premade motifs, so there's no need to cut out your own designs unless you want to. This simplified timesaver makes the project easy for youngsters, and they may alter the doily design by snipping out or adding sections prior to fastening the doilies to their silk screen.

Before affixing the doily, move it around on the screen to find a suitable position. Add other doily sections, creating an over-all pattern which can be reused for repeats. (You can have the design in various colors by running it through a second and third time, cleaning it with tap water between each color run.)

If the design is desired on smaller areas than that of your whole silk screen, simply mask away the borders uniformly with masking tape.

Now put a few drops of rubber cement in a dish, thinning it if necessary with the appropriate thinner. Place the doily face down on a sheet of clean paper and cover its back with cement. Quickly lift it and position it, cemented side down on the screen. Allow it to dry for a half hour or so. Any excess rubber cement may be removed with a clean finger, by gently rubbing it free.

While waiting, get the printing pad and an extra length of fabric ready for a test print. Bear in mind: wherever the doily's solid form appears, the print will be left in the fabric's natural state.

Thinned-down textile colors can be sprayed through paper doilies fastened to screen. Result is shown in illustration at right.

Slip the printing frame over the fabric (hollow frame side up) and tighten the fabric against the working table with some masking tape on its edges. Pour the textile paint into the screen—not too much!—and insert the rubber squeegee which is used to spread the color. Hold it vertically and sweep it back and forth inside the frame until all areas (and the doily) are completely covered with a thin coating of paint. Remove the screen gently upward and your doily print is made. If the test turned out well, go ahead and make your final print. Hang the printed fabric on a clothesline to dry before adding additional colors. When it is dry, press it on both sides with a medium-hot iron. The color will become sun-fast and washable.

Want to reuse the screen? Clean away the rubber cement with carbon tetrachloride or rubber-cement thinner, wash away the color residue with water, and dry the screen. (Be careful when using carbon tetrachloride; it is a volatile poison. Wear rubber gloves and work in a ventilated room.)

If you wish to retain the doily stencil, wash the screen under cold water, working from the inside of the screen. If you plan to discard the stencil, wash it with hot water by holding the frame face up under the tap and rubbing off the doily.

[119]

12

Metalcraft

Working with Tin

As little as twenty minutes' time is your total investment to produce graceful flowers from tin cans! Here's a project that uses as its working material the ends of metal cans from the corner grocery store. You can construct wall hangings, address plates, and decorative centerpieces for your table. Your main tool is a pair of tin snips. You may also need a soldering iron or a blowtorch, although tin flowers can be made without any kind of soldering (see pages 124 and 125).

Begin by sketching your pattern directly on the metal ends which you have removed from the container with a kitchen can opener. (Use the rotating variety which cuts with a smooth, continuous, circle motion.) The drawing is done with a soft lead or grease pencil or china marking crayon. When the motif has been sketched, cut it out with your tin snips. If you prefer to use a coping saw, set the blade with the teeth slanting toward the handle so that all cutting is done on the down stroke. (Do not force the saw—guide it gently around the pattern, and if it should bind, a few rubs of a wax candle across the blade will make it easier to handle.) See photo 1, page 122.

Once the pattern has been cut into the lid, you may add surface decorations by marking its face with a heavy pin, hammered lightly. You can use a door pin, for instance, turning it so the blunt, rounded end is against

Tin snips, tin cans, and a little imagination are all it takes to create novel tin flower decorations for the house.

the metal (photo 2). Place the work on top of a brick or block of wood for greater ease of handling and put a piece of linoleum or a rubber heel beneath it as a cushion.

In creating a leaf design, you will want to add long stems, and 12-gauge copper wire is ideal for the purpose. It is flexible and may be soldered onto the base of the leaf cutout. The soldering procedure is done in the following manner: First, clean the metal pieces with steel wool and apply a coat of paste soldering wax. Then snip a piece of solid wire solder (not acid-core) and position it against the metal leaf's base. Apply heat with a soldering iron. (Or use a blowtorch as shown in photo 3.) If the segments should move out of position during the fusing, push them back together with a bent coat hanger.

If you desire a more stylized shape of leaf, perhaps you will prefer to make the petals of the cutout scraps themselves, soldering these odd-shaped bits onto the main portion. They should be curved by hand before the firing.

The best way to do soldering is to work over a brick or a box filled with sand. This will protect your tabletop from scorching (photo 4). Once you have soldered the stem to the leaves, clean the entire flower form with

[121]

Tin-can flowers designed by June Weaver.

1. Cutting outline of flower from lid of a tin can, using coping saw.

2. Adding surface decoration. Punches and blunt pins of various thicknesses are used with a hammer for this purpose.

3. Wire stems are soldered onto the flowers.

1

3

2

4. A good work surface for soldering is a metal box or pan which can be filled with sand for additional safety. Here it is shown placed over a brick which protects table from heat.

4

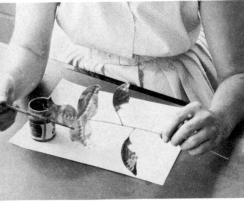

5

5. After polishing metal flowers and leaves with steel wool and wiping them clean they can be painted—or varnished for a shiny natural finish.

steel wool and then wipe it free of dust ready for painting (photo 5). Silver, gold, and black paints are suggested. Avoid garish colors; you are not trying to imitate the real thing. Rather, the purpose is to create flower and leaf forms which take advantage of the inherent beauty of the metal itself. If the stem proves difficult to hold while painting, stick the end into a raw potato or piece of Styrofoam for support.

Your full complement of tools and materials for more complicated projects in tin might include: tin snips and/or coping saw; wax; door pin; 12-gauge copper wire; soft pencil; steel wool; flux and solder; torch; bent hanger; paint and brush.

Making these flowers is child's play, but we do not recommend that young people handle the torch and solder without adequate supervision. For added protection, use asbestos gloves. Your designs are obtained from examining real flowers, gardening books, and magazines and, often, from the border motifs on dinnerware. Best of all, study these ideas, then translate them freely in your own manner.

Two mixed groups of flowers cut from cleaned tin cans and foil pie plates. Individual petals (and leaves) have holes punched at one end for wiring together as flower units. Buttons can be wired for flower centers. Florist tape covers stems. (*From* How to Make Flower Decorations *by Patricia Easterbrook Roberts, courtesy The Viking Press*)

Coat-Hanger Zoo

Using a pair of pliers and a coil of wire, twist yourself an entire menagerie of clever animal shapes which make wonderful decorations for a child's room, for your den or the living-room walls.

Roger Easton, an art instructor with an eye for the bizarre, has developed a simple technique for making wire sculptures at modest expense. Faced with the familiar problem of a large class of students and a low budget, he had to rule out a project with carving wood or modeling clay. But the art theme was "Three-Dimensional Design," and that meant working with materials which could be shaped in the round. What to do?

Three steps in making a simple wire-sculptured duck. Coat hanger or thinner gauge wire can be used. Design is by Roger Easton.

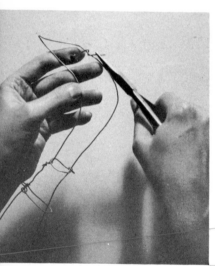

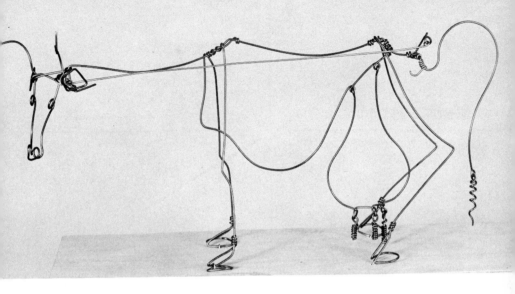

"Cow." Wire sculpture by Alexander Calder. *(Courtesy Museum of Modern Art)*

Coat hangers! The room was filled with them. Could they be twisted into shapes? A bit of experimenting indicated that they were adaptable, but, while the results were adequate, the wire was not sufficiently resilient for intricate work. It was a good introductory project and entirely satisfactory for youngsters. For more intricate work, a moderately pliable wire of 18-gauge annealed, galvanized steel is the ideal solution.

The illustrated examples of Mr. Easton's work were created during a field trip to the local zoo with his students. Finished work like this can be mounted on wooden blocks, hung as wall decorations, or suspended in the form of mobiles.

A commercial-minded hobbyist can find a good market for his wire sculpture among decorators of contemporary homes. A pair of pliers is your only tool in shaping animals of wire. Begin by making pencil sketches. Look at the animal in real life, or in photographs, if necessary. See it from all possible angles. Then distill its form into the predominant "caricature" lines. Boil your sketches down to the absolute minimum of lines. When you are satisfied you have captured the characteristic outline of the animal, you are ready to start twisting wire.

A simple form like a fish may require only four to six feet of wire. (If you want to try using coat hangers, you'll find each one straightens out to about four feet length.) A more complex form may require as much as twenty feet of wire before you are done.

Keep your wire length as long as possible, thus avoiding the need to join pieces too often. When a joint must be made, plan for it to fall at an inconspicuous location—or one in which the twisted joint becomes part of the animal's anatomy. For example, the bend of a leg or arm would be a logical place to join two pieces of wire. The joining is accomplished by twisting the two ends of wire together with the pliers. Crimp them tightly and flat against each other. You will probably lose several inches of wire when making a joint, so hold this waste to a minimum. Avoid unsightly interruptions and bumps along the animal's form.

Details such as eyes, ears, tails, and webbed feet must be stylized interpretations, simplified rather than literal.

Instructions on constructing any of the animals shown would prove superfluous, since each creative individual will prefer to visualize the shape in a personal manner. Study the examples carefully, however, to see how the wire has been handled, the joints planned, and the outlines simplified for rapid recognition.

The form can be balanced on its legs and utilized as a mantelpiece decoration or tablepiece. If you like, you can mount it on a polished wood block, fastening it with heavy staples or U-tacks. Small forms of simple lines (such as a fish) make attractive mobiles, being suspended from the ceiling with black thread. If the form is relatively flat, it can be used as a wall decoration.

While we have talked mostly about animals, there will be readers who prefer to work with abstract shapes. Try twisting geometric shapes, distorted triangles and stars, contorted balls intermixed with other designs. Often, an abstract coiling of wire will create a startling and appealing design. With wire sculpture, *anything goes.*

Working with Sculp-Metal

For years, sculptors have been stymied when it came to making low-cost, permanent renderings of their work. The usual solution was to cast the final clay model in fragile plaster of Paris or permanent bronze. But plaster chips easily and picks up dirt—and who can afford the luxury of bronze casting?

The answer is Sculp-Metal, a plastic substance that looks, feels, and models like clay, but then hardens by itself into a "true" metal that will have all the luster, strength, and permanence of aluminum, bronze, or steel!

Sculp-Metal comes in cans. It is obtainable at art stores and craft supply houses, or may be ordered from the manufacturer, The Sculp-Metal Company, 701 Investment Building, Pittsburgh 22, Pennsylvania. The cost is reasonable.

1

2

3

Wire figure covered with Sculp-Metal. 1. Cut piece of wire twice proposed length of body, including legs. Bend body wire in half; twist together to hips and spread ends out to form legs. Bend to make seated figure. Cut wire length of arms and attach at shoulder height. 2. With palette knife apply ⅛ layer of Sculp-Metal over armature, working into crevices. Keep building up in thin layers. Let harden for a few days. 3. Roughen hardened surface with rasp. Fill in any small pits. Finish filing with half-round file. 4. For finishing touches go over surface with cloth moistened in thinner. Steel wool or buff gives lustrous patina.

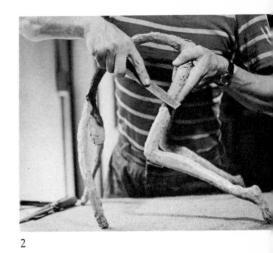

4

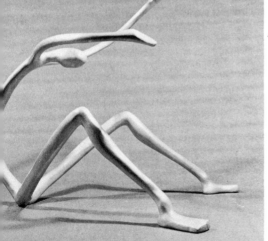

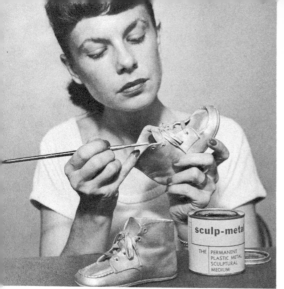

Sculp-Metal may be used for metalizing keepsakes such as leather shoes, baseballs, etc. These baby shoes were made into the bookends shown at right.

Sculp-Metal can be worked with your fingers like ordinary putty, which it resembles in appearance while moist. It can also be applied to preshaped wire armatures or mesh screen shapes with a palette knife, then modeled as desired. Thick masses are built up with thin layers that fuse together. Allow it to stand in the air for a while and it turns metal-hard, after which it can be carved, incised, filed, sanded, or otherwise modeled. Finally, it is buffed and burnished to a rich patina.

The accompanying photos demonstrate two techniques for working in Sculp-Metal. One distinct advantage this medium enjoys is the fact that it is a "direct" modeling procedure. The work you create is itself the finished piece without any necessity for making molds or casts. Duplicates can also be made from your original by conventional means if desired. The Sculp-Metal does not chip, crack, expand, or shrink. It will not rust or corrode when exposed to weather—another advantage over bronze, which usually turns green and dull if placed outside for any length of time. Sculp-Metal withstands temperatures as high as 450° F. without visible effect, and water, grease, or oil will not damage it.

For the hobbyist it is an ideal medium, requiring no heat, flame, flux, or kilns. Schools and workshops should find all these advantages to their liking.

Normally, when Sculp-Metal is polished, it resembles aluminum. It may be made to look like bronze or lead, however, simply by rubbing on some ordinary shoe dye in the hue preferred. The polish is applied and rubbed briskly with a soft cloth to the desired patina; then a protective coating of clear lacquer is sprayed on the finished piece. Readers will enjoy experimenting with other dyes and coloring agents, for the medium is still so new as to offer much exploration.

METALIZING MEMENTOS AND TROPHIES

Yet another use for Sculp-Metal is in metalizing baby shoes, boxing gloves, baseballs, and so on. Here's how you would tackle the job of metalizing a pair of baby shoes. (Follow the same procedure for other objects of like nature.)

First, tie the laces and arrange them neatly. Pull out the tongues to a saucy, realistic angle. Then, using a soft brush (camel's hair is suggested),

"Young Bull." Sculp-Metal figure by Jules Petrancs.

apply Sculp-Metal thinned to a creamlike consistency to the inside and outside of the shoes. About four coats are a good thickness, but allow each coat to dry for a half-hour before applying the next coat. After the four coats have been made, allow the shoes to dry for a day or two. When they are hard and firm to the touch, you may polish them with fine steel wool. This brings out the rich patina of the aluminum base. The finer your steel wool is, the higher will be the gloss. For a mirror-like finish, burnish the shoes, using the back of an old spoon for this procedure.

The finished shoes can be mounted as book ends, used for paper weights, worked into the design of a picture frame, or simply placed on the shelf as a permanent memento.

Gold or bronze finishes are created by the aforementioned rubbing-in of shoe dyes, or with any transparent colored lacquer stocked by your local art supplier.

The tools you will need for working with Sculp-Metal are few. Use tin shears and cutting pliers to shape your armatures—the twisted wire or mesh screen about which the object is to be built. The armature is its skeleton. You'll find use for a rasp, some files, steel wool, and sandpaper, too. These are for lusterizing and incising the metal. A palette knife helps to apply the Sculp-Metal. That's the normal complement of equipment.

We recommend that wire armatures be made of heavy steel clothesline but, in a pinch, you can substitute twisted coat hangers. Mesh screen is preferred when working on larger objects with a hollow core. You can create sculptured pieces as simple as a semiabstract figure made with twisted wire thinly coated with Sculp-Metal, or as complex as a literal head portrait, grouping, or naturalistic animal form. Solid objects may also be decorated with a ball peen hammer to give a hammered metal appearance.

OTHER USES FOR SCULP-METAL

We have been describing Sculp-Metal as a sculptural method; it has many other uses. Automotive designers find it a handy material in creating mock-ups—exact scale models of cars. The Sculp-Metal is mixed equally with its special thinner to make a thin, creamy consistency, and this can then be brushed over the wooden frame of the mock-up model, or painted onto bumpers, trim, and hub caps to impart an aluminum finish. The "wonder metal" is also handy around the house for touching up aluminum trim, screens, planters, bowls, and picture frames. It coats onto any relatively firm material such as leather, canvas, wood, plaster. Model railroaders and plane builders will have obvious uses for it. Home craftsmen can apply Sculp-Metal to candlesticks, boxes, and cigarette receptacles, alchemizing them into handsome gifts. An entirely new field of experience awaits the craftsman who would like to try using the medium to inlay a table. (Just gouge out the wooden surface appropriately and fill with Sculp-Metal.) Once the inlaying is completed, smooth down the surface even to the tabletop with fine sandpaper.

In summation, then, let's list a few important points about using this exciting medium:

1. Build up sculptured figures over rigid wire or hardware screen armatures, to impart strength and create a working skeleton. If the object is large, make a hollow core of mesh screen to save Sculp-Metal.

1. Using ¼-inch mesh screen, cut piece for body; form tube; shape and bind with thin wire. Then make four smaller mesh tubes (from ⅛-inch screening) for arms and legs. 2. Fashion head and neck from ⅛-inch screening. Cut pie-shaped wedges from top of head, then curve remaining tabs together to make crown. Form neck as tube. 3. Fasten head and neck to body; cut hatbrim from screening and wire it to head. Arms and legs are wired to body tube which has been affixed to rough wire armature within it Shoes and hands are made of screen scraps. 4. Daub assembly points

3

4

with Sculp-Metal and let harden. Then cover figure with ⅛-inch layer of Sculp-Metal, building up and modeling features as solid forms. Details are filed and gouged after mixture hardens. Rub with steel wool as final polish.

2. Build up large masses with moderately thin layers (about ⅛ inch) of the material, allowing each layer to dry before progressing to the next. When the modeling is completed, allow object to sit for a few days before filing, burnishing, or finishing. This "curing period" adds strength.

3. To smooth pieces evenly, rub with a soft cloth which has been impregnated in Sculp-Metal thinner.

4. If Sculp-Metal hardens in the container, add thinner until it becomes soft again.

There are two words of caution concerning the use of Sculp-Metal: (1) It is not recommended for casting in molds or applying over oil-base, non-hardening clay. (2) The thinner is inflammable, so work in a well-ventilated room and avoid proximity to open flame.

Decorating with Aluminum Foil

The fellow who saved foil and ended up with a six-foot ball was on the right track, but he was overlooking some wonderful possibilities in creative art! Aluminum foil is the crafts-hobbyist's delight. It is inexpensive, and can be turned into a variety of decorative objects.

Hospital therapy departments are constantly seeking unusual arts and crafts projects which can be prepared by using salvage materials. As a result, scrap aluminum foil in the form of discarded cigarette wrappers, empty pie tins, and frozen-food containers is no longer discarded. The janitor now carefully saves it for the occupational therapist. Patients press it about cardboard containers or empty metal cans, turning out finished items like piggy banks, abstract sculptures, cigarette cases, and gift wraps.

Aluminum foil can be decorated by incising a design or by sgraffito painting. Tools are few—just a stylus, brush, and some Dek-All or Ruxtone Oil Paints.

The photograph shows a jewelry case fashioned from a tin cigarette box, a decorated lid of a tin can, and a plate design rendered on a pie pan, all done by young students.

You can make many other interesting things out of aluminum—lampshades, Christmas-tree ornaments, gift cards, mobiles, and wall hangings. Slipped under a coffee table's glass top, it provides a decorative background. For durability, the colored objects can be baked in a kitchen stove for a few minutes to harden the paint. Even without this step, they will take a good bit of handling without chipping.

When working with aluminum sheeting, sketch the art work on thin paper, then trace it onto the foil with a soft pencil. Colors are applied directly and, if smoother flow is desired, mix a bit of Dek-All Thinner with the paint.

[134]

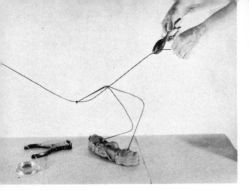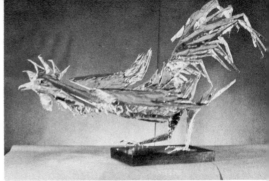

Wire armature forms the skeleton of the cock shown at right. Aluminum-foil wrapping builds up form. Comb and other details can be pasted on or poked through slits made in body.

Finally, you can tackle the problem of textured effect. Press aluminum wrap onto a pebbled book surface or any other textured object. If you have carved linoleum blocks, you can place foil on top and press down with your palm to pick up the impression. This is particularly handy when border repeats or duplicates are desired. Try your hand at aluminum sgraffito—it's a "different" medium.

Group showing decorated pie pan, aluminum-covered cigarette box and lid, and a partly decorated metal can which will later be painted around its side.

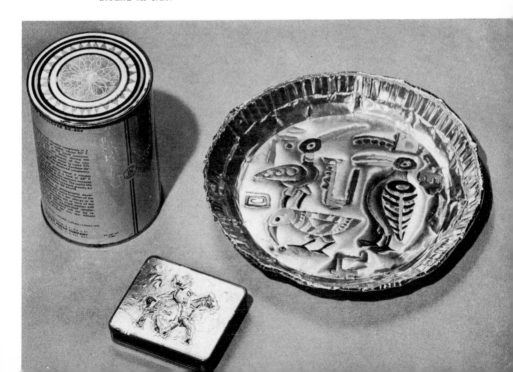

Beautifying Your Home With Metal Painting

Empty cans and attic discards can be brought back to sparkling new life with imagination and oil-based colors. The illustrations show what happened to an empty tobacco tin, some rather gaudy kitchen containers, and a beat-up candle holder. They were given a good cleaning with soap and water, then redecorated, using Dek-All colors. The results: a handsome set of containers for your kitchen shelf and a functionally decorative candlestick to grace your end table or bedroom dresser.

The motifs are selected to suggest the uses to which the objects are to be put. A pencil sketch is traced onto the white (or light-colored) background and the painting done directly on the surface. No complicated procedure is required. It is always easy to decorate if you keep the design simple. If several similar objects are to be duplicated, it may be desirable to trace your motif onto stencil stock and cut out a stencil through which to apply your color. For additional protection and to facilitate cleaning, apply a coat of clear lacquer over the object.

Set of canisters, a tea caddy, and a candlestick —all painted in effective designs that can easily be duplicated.

[136]

13

Mobiles

A SHORT FEW YEARS back, if you'd spoken about mobiles to anyone, you'd have been rewarded with a blank stare, or at most, a quizzically raised eyebrow. The idea was new—actually one of the few innovations in creative art in many years.

Alexander Calder is credited with being its inventor. When his first free-swinging contraptions were exhibited, people were heard to remark: "That's art? My child could do it himself." And so the adults tried it. And it was fun. More, it proved to be a refreshing departure from static art and sculpture, both of which it embodies. These endlessly moving, carefully balanced bits of metal, cardboard, and suspended bric-a-brac provided a real challenge to the maker's ingenuity.

Today, of course, mobiles are respected art forms with innumerable applications. They decorate hotel lobbies and restaurants, spin merrily in contemporary homes and children's nurseries. Posters are designed about their schemes, and advertisements utilize their smart appearance to catch a viewer's hurried eye. They are traffic stoppers.

Constructing a mobile requires few tools. If you work with metal, you'll need a pair of tin snips; otherwise, for cardboard cutting, an ordinary pair of scissors or a razor blade will suffice to slice out the hanging forms. The only other basic equipment and materials are a ball of string or a spool of fine wire, some staples, and paper clips. The hanging segments can be made up of cardboard shapes, metal scraps, balsa, twisted coat hangers, Christmas-tree ornaments—anything that strikes your fancy and will balance the weight of the complementing forms.

A mobile is simply a well-balanced group of suspended shapes. Logically, then, it should be hung where a slight draft or breeze will permit its segments to turn lightly. In order for the mobile to swing freely, the pieces must counterbalance one another so that, as they turn on their axes, they will not touch one another. Here is where much experiment and planning is required of the craftsman. For youngsters, the mobile should have a few simple pieces. More can be added as desired. A good starting project would be a coat-hanger mobile like the illustration here.

Simple Mobiles

The first attempts should be cut from pieces of heavy cardboard—if it is too thin it will warp and make balancing a problem. Geometric shapes (squares, circles, and triangles) provide an excellent introductory project, and this may be followed up by sketching animals and clown faces on cardboard and then cutting around the picture outlines. Don't forget to

Coat - hanger "Spring" mobile features fluttering birds, butterflies caught in a net, and flowers. It is constructed of colored papers, cellophane, a paper cup, costume netting, and small sticks.

Coat - hanger "Circus" mobile. An assortment of cardboard cut-outs are suspended from lengths of #15 wire which serve as mobile's arms. Decorating was done with paint, colored paper, seals, and gummed stars. Other bric-a-brac in the composition are paper cup, cotton-filled cornucopias, and a paper bag.

duplicate the sketch on the reverse side. For surface decoration you may apply a little glue and then sprinkle on metallic powders, bits of cloth, feathers, or anything else that is bright and lightweight. Some other easy suggestions:

Fishmobile. Want something clever and simple enough for a six-year-old to help make? Then cut out some fish shapes, paste on large sequin eyes, a few sparkling bits of glitter for the scales, and then scissor out v-shaped slits along the body to suggest fins and tail. Paint on a few stripes for emphasis. This is the central theme of the fishmobile. Hanging from other adjacent arms you can put abstract shapes, other fishes, even simulated seaweed (of colored bunting paper strips). Bubbles can be simulated with Christmas-tree balls.

Pipe-Cleaner Mobile. Gay little figures can be twisted of colored pipe cleaner, given suits and skirts of fabric scraps and tissue paper. Plan a specific theme and also incorporate appropriate props to dangle alongside the pipe-cleaner "main characters." For instance, a ballet, circus, football team, fairies, goblins. Plan your mobile for holiday purposes.

[139]

Materials for More Advanced Mobiles

Working with metal will create more permanent mobiles. The materials suggested by John Lynch, one of our contemporary masters in the medium (and author of two excellent books on the subject *), include the following:

Cardboard. Get illustrations or poster board in two or more thicknesses. Avoid very thin board, which is liable to warp easily, or too thick a board, which is difficult to cut with a clean edge. The cardboard may be painted in any color or combination of colors you like.

Sheet Metal. Two thicknesses are recommended: .006 "Tagger's tin" and .012 I.C. There are also several heavier weights: .015X, .018XX, .019XXX, and .022XXXX. These are measurements in thousandths of an inch thickness. The first two mentioned, however, may be cut as easily as ordinary cardboard, if you use metal shears. All these tin sheets are available at your local hardware store.

Wire. No. 12, 14, 16, and 19 gauge galvanized iron wire is inexpensive and easy to handle. Hardware stores sell it in one- or five-pound coils at approximately thirty-five cents to forty cents per pound. Don't use aluminum, copper, brass, or steel wire; these are expensive and hard to handle.

Thread. Nylon thread or thin nylon fishing line is strong, lightweight, and attractive.

Paint. Poster paint is good for cardboard mobiles. Use flat oil paint on metal. Have a supply of turpentine on hand whenever you use oil paints, for removing stains and drippings.

ADDITIONAL MATERIALS

Balsa Wood. Use the type that comes in model airplane kits. Wood veneers, too, are manufactured in thin strips which can be shaped and bent. They can be cut with a coping saw.

Plaster of Paris. Can be poured into molds or cardboard boxes to form simple geometric forms. Milk containers, too, make good molds when the plaster of Paris is poured in and hardens. The wax in these containers allows you to remove the hardened form easily.

Plastic. Sheets come in 10 to 20 gauge and are easily cut with ordinary scissors when they are warm (i.e., at room temperature). When colder than average, they are brittle; when too warm, they may sag. Plastic pieces can be glued to one another with acetone, Duco cement or nail-polish remover. Plastic comes in clear finish or in a wide variety of colors.

* *How to Make Mobiles* and *Mobile Design* (New York: Studio Books, The Viking Press).

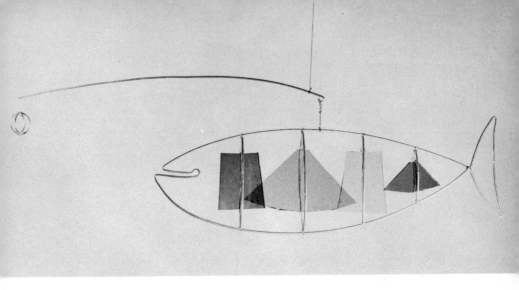

Fish mobile, designed by John Lynch, uses odd scraps of thick colored glass tightly bound with wire. The glass dangles are fastened to the four circles of thicker wire which, in turn, are joined to frame of the fish.

Glass. Try a few experimental mobiles using colored glass. This comes in various colors as sheets measuring 18 inches by 24 inches or larger. Glass is fastened to the arms of a mobile by wrapping the bits with fine wire (26 gauge) and attaching a small wire ring.

The Tools You May Need

Pliers. Long-nosed pliers (3 or 4 inches) with a wire cutter at the side.

Metal Shears. Straight (tinsmith's) or with curved blades especially made for cutting out curves. Use on metal mobiles only.

Scissors. Any heavy-duty type will do for cardboard cutting.

Mat Knife. A handy accessory for cutting sharp angles and more intricate details. on cardboard.

Brushes. Square-tipped camel's-hair brushes are best, and they should be rather large. They are used with tempera colors, water colors, and textile colors, the decorating being rendered on cardboard, paper, or bits of cloth which are glued onto cardboard shapes. Painting on metal is another possibility, and for this purpose use enamel, oil-base paints. (Again, use the water-color brush for the purpose; oil brushes are too stiff.) And finally, if you are an enamelist, you may dust on enamel frit, fire the metal segments, and thus create sparklingly different mobiles.

How to Construct a Mobile

The initial step is to cut out the pieces of cardboard or metal and punch a small hole near the edge of each "shape."

Using pliers, make a small ring of wire and attach this through the hole of the first "shape." Now cut a length of wire to form an arm as shown in photo 1. Bend the tip of the arm into a small hook (attachment loop), and attach your shape to it by the ring. Do the same with your second shape, attaching it by the ring to the other end of the arm.

Next find the balance point as shown in photo 2. A thin piece of string is tied to the arm and moved either to the right or left until the arm is in balance when suspended by the string. When the balance point is found, bend the wire around at this point and continue bending it right around until you have a loop (photo 3).

Now cut a second arm, attach a shape to one end as you did on the first arm. To the other end of the arm, attach first arm by the balance loop you made. Find the balance point on the second arm (which now has a shape on one end and the first arm attached to the other end) and make a balance loop as you did on the first arm. Continue building arms this way until the mobile is the size you want.

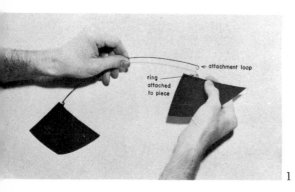

1

3

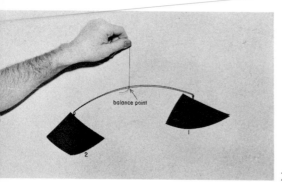

2

Three steps in assembling a mobile, as described above.

Two mobiles. The example above, designed by John Lynch, is made of painted metal shapes; the one at right, called "Flying Geese," is by Franklin Rich, who cut the shapes out of balsa wood.

14

Hand Puppets and Dolls

T HE COLORFUL little people illustrated here and in color on page 149 are simply broomsticks in disguise.

The body is a tiny broom, the kind sold in toy stores. A neck is fashioned by wrapping masking tape an inch thick and two inches deep at the point where the handle joins the straws. Doll arms are next affixed to an upper torso made of adhesive-backed outing flannel which has been built up around the top of the straws like a vest. The arms are taped and locked inside this material until they will not pull free, but can be rotated at will. (Another possibility: make the doll arms from a twisted wire coat hanger. The hanger is looped tightly across the doll's "chest" or neck, then bent into position and covered with papier-mâché stripping to simulate flesh after painting.)

The legs are made by cutting away the broomstraws from the bottom until just two columns are left which can be wrapped with outing flannel, forming the lower appendages. The remainder of the broomstraws—about whiskbroom size—is left as an upper portion which serves as the doll's middle. In female dolls, this will resemble a petticoat of straw. For male dolls, simply divide the broomstraws into two equal halves and bind each with outing flannel into the leg shapes.

Feet are built up with more flannel padding and have soles made of Band-Aid adhesive. The flannel can be dyed to simulate shoes, with colored inks or liquid shoe polish.

Next comes the head—and it can be interchangeable so that the puppet can assume several identities with a flick of your hand. It is a regular rubber doll's head, but the innocuous, store-bought appearance of the face is changed by circling it with papier-mâché stripping and masking tape. With the original face thus blanked out, you can create a new one with real personality. Face, arms, and legs can be decorated with a special mixture made up of equal parts of powder tempera and liquid starch. (You may also use premixed tempera colors for smaller, individual projects.) The starch helps bind the tempera to the papier-mâché and tape. Finer details can be added with water color.

The decorated head is now ready to be mounted in position. It already has a hole for the neck, but you must now cut another small opening on top. Make it a little smaller in circumference than the broomstick handle, for, being made of rubber, the hole in the doll's head will stretch, assuring a snug fit. Slip the head down the broomstick and onto the masking-tape neck you constructed as the first step. It will hold firm, yet it can be removed without difficulty.

The broomstick puppet is ready to dress. Clothing is the same standard doll's garments which all toy shops stock. You can also pick up little props at the five-and-dime store—miniature hatboxes, doll-size glasses, shoes, imitation flowers, and such things. Or, if you'd like to keep it entirely your own doing, cut the clothing from Indian Head cloth and fabric scraps.

The puppets are fun to play with. Children can fashion a theater from a large empty cardboard carton—the kind major household appliances or TV sets are packed in—paint the broom handle the same color as the stage's background, and remain out of sight on stools while manipulating their puppet friends.

Materials for broomstick puppets include: doll's clothes, child's broom, masking tape, and papier-mâché. Decorating on coarse fabric is done with liquid starch mixed with tempera powders. For smooth fabrics use regular fabric paint.

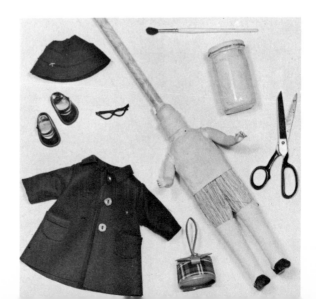

Hobbyhorse Sock Puppets

Rags, an old sock, a broomstick handle; put them together and you have a fiery steed that's galloping good fun for any imaginative youngster.

Hobbyhorses are child's play to construct, and the motif can be anything under the sun. Did we say hobbyhorse? Perhaps we mean hobby-creatures, for there's no reason why you can't ride off on a lion, clown, or man-from-Mars. They're all made the same way: a stocking is filled with rags, cotton, or straw, packed tightly enough to provide a solid form for easy handling. The neck is joined with masking tape or friction tape to a sawed-off broomstick, and then the design is added.

For painting on features, we suggest a mixture of liquid starch and powder tempera. This flows on easily and adheres to the stocking surface. You can then add sewed-on sequins, buttons, bits of scrap fabric, a mane of knitting yarn (an old mop will do). If you wish to provide reins, attach long shoestrings. Paint the broomstick with enamel paints, and the job is completed.

Hobbyhorses make fine party favors and are salable items for your school or church bazaar.

Youngsters love to create practical toys—things they can use and not simply look at. Why not take your corral of horses and stage a playtime rodeo in a recreation area? Need a corral to house your livestock? A bale of chicken wire or snow fence (borrowed from the school janitor or contributed from a sympathetic hardware dealer) will do nicely.

Hobby-horse broomstick puppet—shown also in detail opposite. An old, stuffed stocking makes the head; decorations include odd bits of yarn, felt, and ribbon.

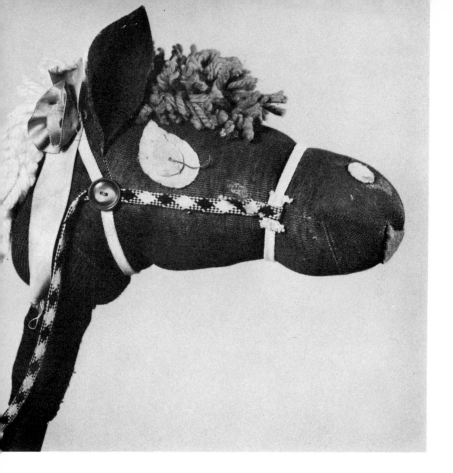

Stuffed Toys and Dolls

Anyone who is handy with a needle and thread can make unusual dolls to rival the highest-priced variety and often to surpass them in originality and practicality. On these pages you'll find a collection made by Betty Gage, a young homemaker who never knew she had any artistic talent until she received a sewing machine for Christmas. Within a few weeks she abandoned the pattern motifs and struck out on her own. The first few went to friends; then, when the word got around, Betty was deluged with orders for rag dolls, cushions, and assorted gifts. Within a few months she had created over two hundred of them and launched herself in a profitable business.

The Gage dolls now sell for three dollars and upward. The cash outlay to create them is under fifty cents for materials. These consist of kapok or cotton for stuffing, scrap fabrics and Indian Head cloth for the covering and accessories, and textile colors for features. Eyes are usually buttons or cloth scraps sewn on, mouths are red cloth, skin coloring is either dyed fabric or Prang textile colors. In some cases, doll accessories can be incorporated, purchased at any local five-and-dime store.

At the other end of the time pendulum is the work of a septuagenarian grandmother named Mrs. William Albrecht. What does a widow of seventy-two do with her spare time? Rocking chairs never appealed to Mrs. Albrecht, so she decided to create hand puppets for the children in the neighborhood. She, too, found her output salable and made of it a tidy little business venture. Her motifs are largely animals—snorting horses with yarn manes, giraffes, and calico roosters—a barnyard of lively things which can be slipped over your hand and manipulated to delight small fry. The construction details are obvious; you'll find them under the illustrations.

Basic materials for doll-making include needle and thread, scissors, Indian Head cloth, textile colors and brush, yarn for hair, and scrap fabrics for costuming and stuffing.

Broomstick puppets. *(See also page 144.)*

A trio of scrap-pile hand puppets, stuffed with cotton and inexpensive ground foam rubber. Decorations include bits of string, yarn, felt, sequins, buttons. *(Courtesy Freda Harrington, Wayne University)*

Giraffe and sort-of-poodle hand puppets were created out of odds and ends by Mrs. William Albrecht.

15

Stone Decorating

Talking Stones

Horace Crist has been picking up pebbles from the beach for years and decorating them with fanciful colors to match their naturally unusual shapes. It's quite a game, studying an eroded rock and visualizing it as an angry old man, a fierce Indian warrior, a prehistoric monster, or an abstract three-dimensional design.

Decorated stones—Crist calls them "talking stones" because they tell him stories about themselves, which he translates for those who are hard of hearing—make excellent paper weights, book ends, table pieces, and doorstops.

The equipment for preparing and decorating these stones is simple. The working kit consists of textile or oil colors, India ink (for drawing on the design and then adding emphasis after painting), a hammer and chisel for shaping, a block of wood for mounting, some glue to fasten the stone to its wood base, and some varnish as a protective finish.

Walk down the beach or stream bed and it is never long before an interestingly shaped stone or pebble is discovered. Pick it up, turn it around in your hands, and examine it from various angles to discover its basic shape. What does it suggest? A voodoo doll? Clown? Just an exciting abstract form? Decide on the theme, and you're ready to go to work.

Stonecraft designs by Horace Crist.

First, clean the stone with scouring powder to remove the grit and prepare the surface for paint. Once this is done, begin sketching directly on the surface, using a brush or pen dipped in India ink. Work boldly, avoiding elaborate detail. As soon as the ink dries, you can start applying brightly colored paints.

If, prior to decorating, certain portions of the stone seem superfluous, remove these areas with a chisel or coarse sandpaper.

Once the paint dries, the stone should be varnished against wear. The final step is to mount the stone. Select a piece of redwood or some similar wood with an attractive color and grain, saw this into a size that will balance the stone properly, and then gouge out a groove into which the base of it will fit securely. Pour in some transparent cement and then insert the decorated stone, removing any adhesive which runs out of the groove. Allow the stone to set overnight, then give both the stone and the block a light coat of varnish.

This interesting project is recommended for any imaginative craftsman who, bending an ear to a rock pile, can hear the stones begging to be turned into something useful and unusual.

Opposite: Equipment for stone painting consists of oil paints or tempera, brushes, drawing ink for finer details, and varnish for a permanent shiny finish. Hammer and chisel are useful for shaping stones. *(Photo courtesy Horace Crist and* Design *Magazine)*

Right: Group of hand-painted stones. *(Courtesy Binney and Smith)*

More of Horace Crist's talking stones.

Flotsam Collages

An old sculptor has been on the job since the dawn of prehistory. His name is erosion, and he concentrates his efforts on weathering stones and bits of driftwood. On these pages you'll find some prime examples of his handiwork, as translated by imaginative young artists under the direction of teacher Paul Williams.

During an outing along the banks of Lake Erie, these pre-high-schoolers picked up interestingly shaped pebbles, mounted them on cardboard, and applied some freehand sketching to create appropriate backgrounds for their pebblecraft portraits. Our beachcombers saw dashing ponies, storks acting as mailmen, and sophisticated boulevardiers. Many of their examples now decorate playrooms and living rooms. A simple picture frame with the glass removed can add the finishing touch to this novel experiment.

[156]

Stones, pebbles, and bits of wood are pasted on decorated cardboard mounts to form these colorful collages.

16

Mosaic Craft

Iᴛ ᴏᴜ ᴡɪsʜ to make a mosaic, *get involved*. Throw off your preconceived notions about beauty. What you produce may not be great art—it may not be art at all, but it will reveal in its very awkwardness a kinship with things lovable. And do not care if your friends laugh at your handiwork. A world that is saturated with trite formulas for beauty sometimes does not know how to act in the presence of the real thing.

Here are some experimental ideas in the making of original mosaics. The process of making a mosaic is called *tessellating*. Just as a painter paints, so, as a mosaic maker, you will spend your time tessellating.

Mosaic Materials

Each little piece in a mosaic is called a tessera (from the Latin, meaning "small piece"). The tesserae are derived by cutting bits from clay or domestic unglazed tile, or by fitting together chunks of glass. When

Opposite: Making a mosaic tabletop. In areas using any large amount of cement or adhesive, wire mesh (see foreground) is embedded to prevent surface from cracking after drying. Colored tesserae (chipped tiles) are laid in patterns according to pre-planned design. (*Photo from* Mosaics for Everyone *by Sister Magdalen Mary*)

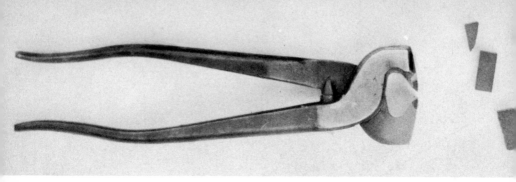

Tool for cutting and shaping tiles for mosaic designs.

these bits are assembled, they create a pattern which may be a literal depiction or a pure abstract design.

Unglazed domestic tile is available at most artcraft shops in about thirty muted colors. It is made from high-fire clay. Venetian glass is also available in sheets and may be used for your projects. It is easier to cut than clay tile but is somewhat more expensive.

The cutting is done with tile cutters. It takes a good amount of pressure to cut tile, but an easier method is to nibble away the edges with a tool or, on larger pieces, score the tile with the cutter blade and then break the unwanted pieces free.

It is not always necessary to cut and snip your tesserae painstakingly to fit a preconceived shape. The simplest way to produce a good quantity of tesserae is to place tiles between two pieces of cardboard and strike them several times with a hammer or wooden mallet.

Flat Mosaics

Generally speaking, the steps in creating a flat mosaic for inlaying tabletops making plaques or constructing murals are as follows:

1. Draw your design on tracing paper, then transfer it to a sheet of plywood, rendering it in India ink. This becomes your working surface.

2. The tiles are then fastened onto the design sketch with tile adhesive. (Miracle Adhesive is one we can recommend.) A small space is left around each tessera.

3. The mosaic is then completed by grouting between the bits to the level of the tesserae. Use finger tips or any burnishing tool for this. Grout is commercially available, or you may use cement if the mural will be used outdoors or as a floor inlay. Wipe off the excess grout with a damp rag. If residue portions are discovered after drying, these may be scraped off with a razor.

Mosaic mural project executed entirely by children. (*Courtesy Sister Magdalen Mary of the Immaculate Heart College, Los Angeles*)

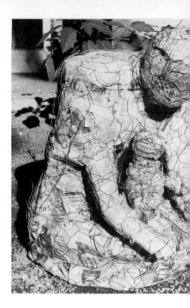

Mosaic sculpture begins by building up form with papier-mâché. Chicken-wire covering adds strength. Object is then given two-inch-thick coat of Magnesite compound and tesserae are pressed in position. Mosaic is derived from broken bits of green ginger-ale bottles set in black Magnesite.

Mosaic Sculpture

This procedure is followed when working on flat surfaces, as for a tabletop or a wall hanging. A somewhat different method is required in making a mosaic sculpture. Here you will begin, perhaps, by preparing a small-sized model in clay. Then, with this as a guide, you can rough up the shape full size with an inner core of cardboard cartons tied together. The shape is completed by tying crushed or rolled newspapers around this core. On top of this you add three or four layers of newspaper strips (full length) dipped in wheat paste to create the medium known as papier-mâché. When the paste dries, cover the form with chicken wire and tie it firmly in place, thus making a sturdy armature about which to add your tesserae.

The figure is now covered with mosaic adhesive. (We prefer a brand named Magnesite.) Begin by spreading it at the base of the figure and work up to a height of five or six inches. Then, press in your tesserae and allow them to set before working higher on the figure.

Just how long the setting requires is hard to predict, but do not rush ahead impatiently or the tesserae weight will cause the sculpture to sag. Your coating of adhesive should be at least an inch thick for small figures, and perhaps double that for larger ones. The technique progresses in this manner to completion. Keep viewing the sculpture from various angles as you work, making corrections before the tesserae harden in place. As a final step, grouting compound is worked in between the individual tiles to form a strong, unified piece of mosaic sculpture.

The finished mosaic sculpture "Madonna and Child" by Joan Gabriel. *(Photo Courtesy Immaculate Heart College, Los Angeles)*

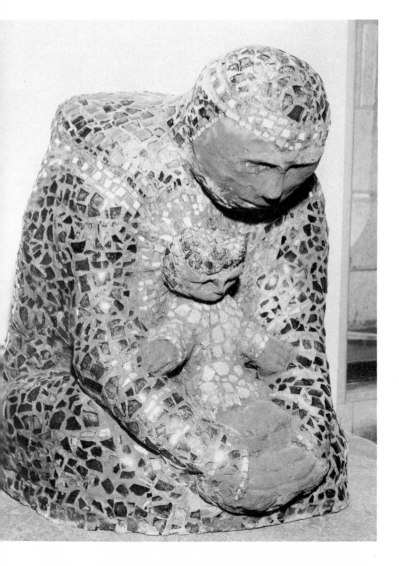

Types of Adhesive for Various Purposes

Miracle Adhesive is used to fasten tesserae to vertical surfaces. It will hold the pieces in place without danger of sliding, even before the adhesive has set. The adhesive is produced by the Mosaic Tile Company.

Duco Cement (a product of Du Pont) is used to fasten glass to glass. It is transparent, can be purchased in tubes at stationery stores, five-and-ten-cent stores, and most hardware shops. (You might like to try an interesting "stained glass" experiment with this material, joining bits of broken glass and bottle scraps to windowpanes. In buying panes, get scratched plate glass; it is quite inexpensive because of its flaws, and these are covered anyway.)

Magnesite (short for magnesium oxychloride cement) is used to adhere tesserae to a paper foundation. It is applied thickly—from an inch to two inches in thickness. Suppliers may know this as Sorrell Cement or Woodstone. For additional information on this product consult your local chemical supply houses or write to The Oxychloride Cement Association, Connecticut Avenue, Washington, D.C. It is reasonably waterproof, but prolonged submersion in water will cause it to deteriorate. It is often used for outdoor stairways and building murals, as well as for sculpture made over papier-mâché. Store it in a dry place, and mix the stock Magnesite with magnesium chloride solution to form a paste. It is neutral in color, and thus you must add a small amount of alkali-proof color to reach the hue you want.

Because of its great weight, Magnesite requires a supporting armature of chicken wire to be placed about the sculpture form. Try to match or complement the color of the tesserae with the Magnesite color—that is, for dark green tesserae, set the bits in dark green, dark gray, or dark red Magnesite. If it accidentally splashes or runs over your tiles, it may be removed with commercial tile cleaner.

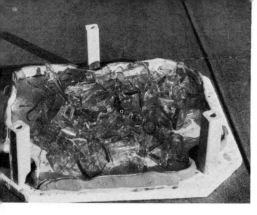

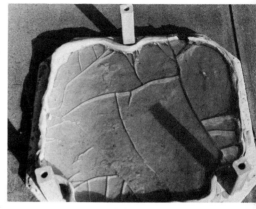

Opposite page and above: Old bottles can be broken up and used for tésserae. Flat pieces of colored glass can also be made by firing old bottles in a kiln. Clay wall about ½ inch high should be built to keep melted glass bottles from flowing off shelf. Glass hardens flat and can be cut for tesserae and other purposes such as stained glass or shapes in a mobile as shown on page 141. *Below:* Beads, badges, and other objects also suggest unusual mosaic-type decorations. Old pipes were used here for experimental effects. *(Photos Courtesy Immaculate Heart College, Los Angeles)*

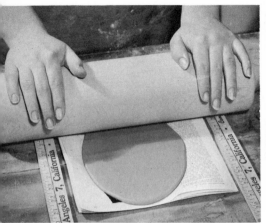

Making a clay mosaic. Place a wedge of clay between two rulers and roll it flat to create a slab *(left)*. Then, using a colored glaze, paint the soft clay. When dry cut slab into small squares of varying sizes and shapes *(right)* to use as tesserae for mosaic pictures.

Simple Projects for Young People

Make your own tesserae by rolling low-fire clay with a rolling pin, slicing it with a knife into strips and then into pieces, and firing the fragments in a ceramic kiln. (See Chapter 8.)

Purchase glazed bathroom tiles from a local building supply store and then break these with a hammer (between cardboard, to prevent marring or dangerous flying fragments). They usually come in perhaps a half-dozen basic colors—yellow, white, black, green, blue, rose. While first-grade bathroom tile is expensive, damaged pieces cost little or nothing. Children can make simple mosaics with them. Murals may be constructed by children, working on plywood with Wilhold Glue. It is best to cover the plywood with this glue on both sides and the edges a day or so before starting the mural. This will prevent the board from warping. The glue is sold commercially in a squeeze-type Glu-Bird container. If you plan on doing a lot of mosaic projects you will find it economical to buy the Wilhold Glue at lumber yards in five-gallon drums and then refill the dispensers as required. It is particularly good for mosaic table construction, and you may supplement your kitchen-tile tesserae with other bits cut out from linoleum, if desired. Children might also enjoy experimenting at the lowest possible cost by making their murals on nothing more than heavy cardboard.

Ox mosaic built over welded steel frame by Sahl Swarz. The figure is 27 inches long.

Simple objects used in the photo opposite.

17

Creative Photography

New World Through a Glass Block

WHAT IN THE WORLD—or out of it—are the strange shapes on the opposite page? They are simply bits of colored paper and such props as a pencil, paint jar, string, and similar oddments, viewed through a glass block. Peer glass blocks are available from building suppliers and department stores at very little cost. These blocks distort whatever lies behind them and are commonly used to allow light to enter building without the distraction of the literal world that is beyond. Buy two of them and let the blocks double as book ends in between your experiments in photography.

There are hours of entertainment and valid inspiration for designers locked up in a block of hollowed-out glass. For photographers it provides something different in viewing the workaday world and, properly positioned before a sitter, it can create a fascinating caricature portrait. For the artist, the glass block is an entree to a bewildering world of distorted shapes, colors, and tonal values.

A glass block can be put to practical use in discovering the elements of abstract design, for it effectively eliminates the crutch of seeing things recognizably, and instead makes the viewer think in terms of design for its own sake.

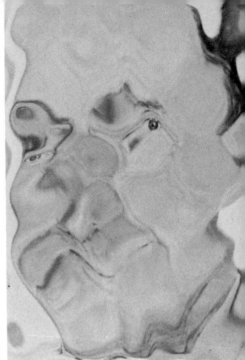

Magazine cover seen through glass
block becomes an amusing caricature.

Take a magazine cover, a photograph, or even hold the block up before
a window, and the fun begins! By resting the block in a handy position,
you can view the scene caught in its face and sketch a freshly different
still life. A vase of flowers becomes a jungle of twisted, graceful shapes;
a windowpane's wooden cross supports twist and weave like scattered
strings. Pencils turn to rubber, a hand dissolves to sausage, even a jar of
rubber cement and a teacup become gaping-mouthed beasts intent on
devouring each other. Youngsters love this ever-changing sideshow.

Although the illustrated examples were photographed for reproduction,
the discerning viewer can easly sketch or paint what he sees. It is important that you remain in the same position during any sketching, for
the slightest change of the point of view will completely alter the pattern
created.

Photograms

Anyone can produce photograms. They are pictures made without a
camera, the result of exposing photographic paper to light, with opaque
and transparent objects resting against the paper.

You will soon discover fanciful shapes in commonplace objects, weird

Abstract photo design entitled "Guitarist at Work." Objects
used are strands of colored yarn against a piece of black paper.

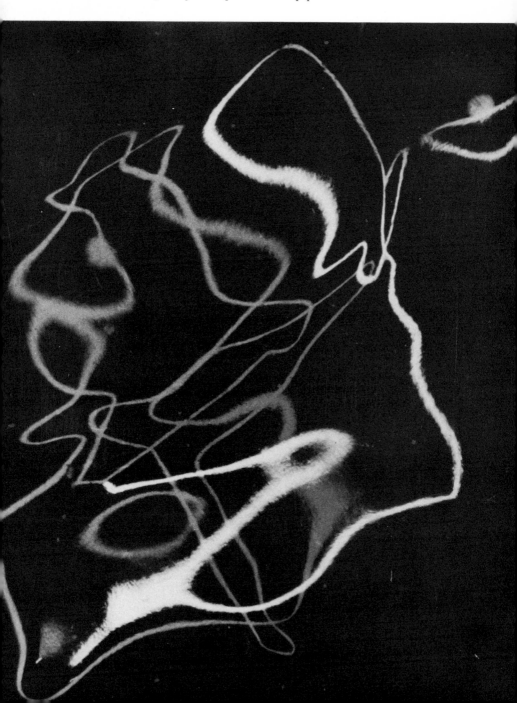

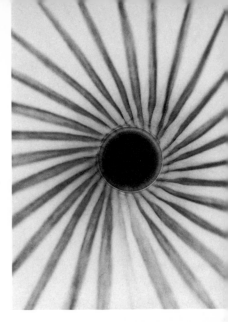

An imaginative photograph of a glass pickle jar seen from below. (*Courtesy Michael Kosinski*)

and beautiful designs hidden in the silhouettes of beads, leaves, glasses, wire screening, and countless other household articles.

For a few dollars you can obtain the necessary supplies from your local photo supply dealer. These consist of developer, fixer, and a package of 8-inch-by-10-inch photo paper.

The procedure

Place an object on a sheet of photo paper in a darkened room or closet equipped with a photographer's safelight. This light, available at photo supply stores, will enable you to see your work without fogging the paper before exposure. Then, lighting a hundred-watt bulb a foot away from the paper, expose the work for a few seconds. Wherever the object touches the paper, it will cast its shadow or otherwise screen out light. This silhouette (or semisilhouette, depending on the light-blocking capacity of the object) will be cast on the paper. Areas not so blocked will turn black when developed; those screened will remain white or some degree of gray tone.

The exposed paper is immersed in developer for a minute and a half, or until the image comes through to your satisfaction. It is then dipped in water to wash off the developer, and afterward immersed in the hypo (i.e., fixing) bath, which neutralizes the final traces of developing chemical and makes the image permanent. After fixing, the photogram is completed and is placed in running water for a half-hour to wash away the hypo. Place between blotters to dry, with a slight weight on top to prevent curling, and you have produced a photogram.

Any object is fair game for a photogram: paper clips, torn cardboard, brushes, talcum powder. Powder, salt, or sugar will cast minute shadows that become falling snow when development is made. Cut out silhouettes: make skyscrapers, boats, portraits, trees, mountains. Cut glass casts unusual shadows and light areas. Straws and toothpicks produce odd geometrical shapes. You can combine dozens of objects to create striking photograms. These can have practical applications, such as greeting cards, posters or bookplates.

A piece of sandwich-spread glass photographed in detail makes a dramatic swirling pattern. (*Courtesy Michael Kosinski*)

Right: In this photogram, pine twigs fall into a natural, free-flowing pattern. (*Courtesy Michael Kosinski*)

Left: A leaf takes its own X-ray portrait when bright light flashes down to silhouette it against photo paper.

Flashlight Pendulum Designs

A piece of string, a camera, and a flashlight in a darkened room—put them all together and the result is a unique experiment in unpredictable design.

To the uninitiated eye, a flashlight swinging back and forth describes a simple arc. But set your camera for a time exposure, open its eye in the dark, let the flashlight swing in front of the lens for a minute or more, and you'll come up with strange and beautiful light patterns, similar to the one on the opposite page.

As the light swings on its string, it fights a continuing battle with inertia. Each swing is a little smaller, each movement a trifle slower. These changes of arc and speed are captured by the camera and left as streaks across its film. No two pendulum designs will ever be exactly alike.

The procedure is simple, and you can take your pictures with almost any kind of camera, for the flashlight beam is bright enough to register on even a pinhole lens. If you have no darkroom available, just send the film to your photo finisher for development and printing. Here's the technique:

1. Hang your flashlight on a string from the ceiling of a darkened room. (You may use a bright light bulb on a long extension cord if you wish.) Set up your camera on a tripod or tabletop, pointed directly at the light source. The distance from light to camera should be sufficient so that the widest point of the arc will not go beyond the area seen by the camera. In most cases, six feet is about right.

Flashlight pendulum design.

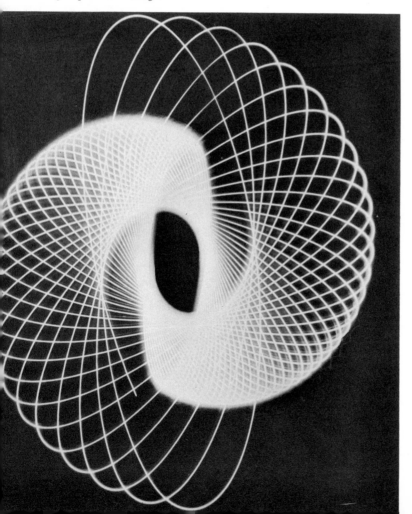

Photostat gift box made by Jerry White.

2. Set your camera to a small aperture and on time. Give the light a good swing and let it move back and forth a few times to establish a steady arc. Then trigger your camera and expose for anywhere from a few moments to a minute, depending on the complexity of the design desired.

3. You may swing the light for a short time, cover the camera lens (with black tape or a lens shade) and then stop the swinging movement and start it again in a different direction. From here on, there is no way to predict the results. Try varying experiments, shooting from directly below, from the sides, with more than one light source, or even working with color film and different colored lights.

Photostat Gift Boxes

Take one empty cardboard box, add an artistic photostat enlargement, and the result will be a distinctive gift box.

Here is a fine opportunity to combine your photographic prowess with package designs that are personalized to suit every occasion. Holiday themes in season, gay cartoons, and original artwork reproduced in fade-proof, smudgeproof, photostat form—an endless variety of uses and the mechanical labor is confined to Scotch-taping the art in position!

Photostat paper is recommended because of its adaptability for creasing and folding. (Photographic enlarging paper is more prone to crack.) Photostat enlargements are very moderate in cost, and any blueprint house or photo supply store will make them for you. And many art suppliers will, too.

Even if you aren't handy with a camera, you can make these motifs, for a photostat will reproduce original artwork, maps, a layout of labels, collages—just about anything that is bold and emphasizes the black and white tones rather than subtle grays. Just take your design to the photostat house and they'll deliver finished prints in twenty-four hours.

To cover box, photostat is placed face down on table and box lid centered over it. Paper is then creased over edges and firmly Scotch-taped down along inside edges of lid.

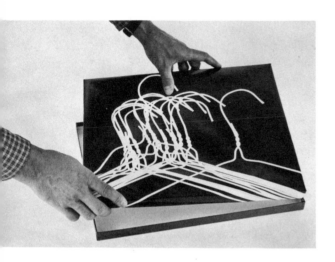

Photostat coat-hanger-box design, made as described on page 172.

Let us assume you wish to present a book or album to someone. What is the theme of the book? Cooking? Then a collage of vegetable silhouettes, a magazine illustration of kitchenware, or a photograph of yourself at work in your kitchen would prove most appropriate. Or is it a snapshot album for the grandparents of your youngsters? Then try your hand at some cartoon artwork of children at play, possibly combining it with a photograph of alphabet blocks. Then photostat it or have it done for you.

Have you a favorite textured fabric? Paste it flat on a cardboard and reproduce it. A distinctive holiday gift wrap you would like to incorporate into this more permanent form? Photostat it. Using the original material lacks uniqueness, but once it has been photostated it becomes a completely new entity, and one upon which you can add varying forms of decorative design without any danger of their tearing free.

Your tools are equally simple: a ruler and sharp blade for trimming the stat to size, Scotch tape and scissors for fastening the folded edges to the inside of the box lid.

18

Hand-Decorated Boxes

THE DISTINCTIVE CONTAINERS which illustrate this section were all made by amateurs, yet they rival the most costly gift items in quality and appearance. The uses to which they may be put are manifold; they may hold cigarettes, jewelry, candies, stationery—oddments of your own choosing—and they make wonderful containers for gifts.

The materials required for their construction are easily available, consisting of little more than the basic box, decorating art supplies, a few common art tools, and a can of plastic spray or clear lacquer.

Children can invent their own original designs, drawing directly on the box cover or on paper which can then be glued on the lid. The medium in which they work is not important—wax crayon, water color, tempera, colored felt-tip pens, enamel paints. Some of our examples were done by children of three to six, others by older children and adults.

The procedure (it is quite flexible) can follow these suggested lines:

1. Obtain a quantity of undecorated, unpainted wooden boxes which are adaptable to the use for which the finished product is intended. A typical supplier (and the one from which our own samples were obtained) is the O-P Craft Company, Sandusky, Ohio. Their boxes range in size from 3 x 3½ x 2 inches at around half a dollar in cost to 4½ x 10½ x 2½ inches at a little over a dollar. Also available are unfinished boxes with

Gift box with folk-art-type design,
painted with tempera (poster) paints.

six compartments and a handy recipe file box. It is also quite possible to utilize empty cigar boxes and similar discards, the only requisite being that the paper wrappers be removed for better preparation. (Gummed labels can be soaked off with a warm, damp rag, but be careful not to warp the wood during this procedure.)

2. The next step is to plan your design, working on tracing paper if you wish to transfer the motif later rather than render it freehand. Draw the design exact size, perhaps allowing a quarter-inch margin on each side so that the painted wood of the box will become a neat border.

3. Now you are ready to prepare the box for rendering. If art is to be done directly on the cover, first give the entire lid a coating of semi-gloss white enamel. (Any other color may be used, but most of our examples are in white.) You may also coat the whole box with semi-gloss, but if the lid is detachable it is preferable to use a stain or varnish on the rest of the container, leaving only the cover in contrasting white.

4. If this is to be a child's project—an attempt to perpetuate his freehand art just as he draws it—the child may now draw directly on the box

[179]

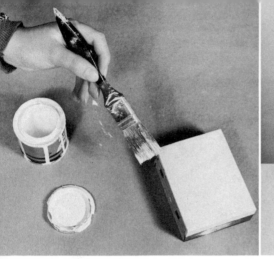

Unpainted box should be given two coats of paint. Use semi-gloss paint when design is to be rendered in tempera, felt-tip pen, or oils; use flat paint when crayons or colored pencils are to be used for drawing over the background. Youngster at right excitedly started her design before completing background color on sides. More fun at first, but it makes it harder to achieve a smooth, even match later on.

lid with crayon. If crayons or colored pencils are used, the lid should be painted with flat white paint, so that the hard leads will adhere to the surface. If colored felt-tip pens such as the Cado-marker or Flo-master are used, these can be applied onto almost any type of painted or stained surface, and tempera colors are similarly versatile. Original water colors are not rendered on the box lid proper, but are done on water color paper, then are cut out to size and glued to the lid.

5. When the artwork is completed and dry, the box lid (or entire box) is given several coats of clear lacquer or plastic spray to seal in the handwork permanently and to make future cleaning a simple matter.

These are not the only ways to decorate boxes. Another fascinating project requires no freehand art at all—just the use of scissors or an X-acto knife and straight-edge ruler. In this approach, bits of colored construction paper, fragments of printed advertising, typography, or pre-printed artwork are cut from magazines, books, and other sources, laid on the box lid and arranged into a pleasing design, then cemented in place over the white background. To protect the printed art from smudging and the grime of use, a sheet of clear plastic is cut to size and fixed over the artwork. You may glue tiny strips of molding around the edges, or employ the smallest of nails for this purpose, thus holding the clear plastic sheet tight against the original or reproduced artwork.

Some suggested sources of excellent pre-printed design motifs: illustrations from children's paperback books and low-cost larger books; advertisements from magazines; editorial illustrations from magazines and gravure-printed newspapers; printed wallpaper.

The use of lacquer, shellac, or plastic sprays is not recommended over pre-printed artwork simply because most such work has been printed on both sides and the lacquer or spray will make it relatively transparent by soaking into the fibers. This makes the reverse printed side visible. If the reproduction has not been printed on both sides, you can spray or lacquer it, but first do some experimenting with unimportant scraps.

Your decorated boxes can also feature fine art reprints, prepared in the manner earlier described.

Color reproductions cut from magazines, or original water colors, or oils rendered on paper may be cut out and positioned on box lids. Use rubber cement, applied to both the box and back of art, for fastening.

Designs are protected by a coating of clear plastic or lacquer spray. Or simply brush on a coat of clear varnish.

Breadboard stencil-decorated by Art Tanchon.

19

Decorating on Wood

Antiquing

PRODUCING AN ANTIQUE reproduction is a creative undertaking that can range far beyond mere copywork. The true craftsman accepts it as a challenge which involves careful research, constant experimentation, tactile facility, and planning. The end results can thus be honest interpretations of fine craftsmanship of another day, or just obvious imitations. It's up to you.

Too often a woodworking hobbyist comes to believe that if a piece has that beaten-up look, it is certain to resemble an antique. Nothing is further from the truth. Excessive distressing of an object is obvious to any viewer and imparts an artificial appearance.

In this section, we're going to explore the professional's "tricks of the trade," but bear in mind that these are aids rather than automatic steps. The reproduction of a Colonial antique (for this is the type we will analyze) means turning back the clock, resorting to contemporary technique simply because it saves much time and reaches the same end result without sacrificing fidelity.

Many an *aficionado* feels it is essential to use aged wood—old bits from a weatherbeaten attic or perhaps old orange crates. It is quite possible, however, to use ordinary, unpainted furniture and do your own aging with tools and stains. As in any art project, restraint is the proper approach, rather than overindulgence.

USING A KNIFE

Most of the important work in antiquing can be done with a sharp knife. It will be used to round the edges and corners, simulating the handling of many years. One blade would not be sufficient. You should have a good handle that is designed to hold various types of blades interchangeably.

Work slowly or on small sections. Where an extremely deep cut is required by your work, use several short gouges rather than trying to rip out all the wood at one time. Remember, you're interested in duplicating the passage of time, not just chopping chunks away. Always use short, sweeping strokes, cutting with the grain of the wood. On those occasions where it does become necessary to cut against the grain, pause to resharpen your blade and then, pressing lightly, cut out a little at a time. Proper sanding is the next important phase. Never use coarse sandpaper. Start with grade 2/0 paper and finish the sanding with either grade 4/0 or 6/0. Again, as with cutting, sand with the grain. Hold the paper in your palm so that you will produce a natural, curved surface.

DUPLICATING WORM TRACINGS

Worm tracings can be produced with thin wire and a hammer. Hand-form the wire so that it is not straight and hold it firmly over the wood surface to be treated. Now tap the wire gently with a hammer so that it forms an impression on the wood. This impression should not be uniform in depth. Vary it. And be sparing. Only a few worm tracings to any one surface.

AGED DENTS AND SCARS

Using a piece of hardwood block, turn it so that one edge or face is against the work, and then strike it lightly with a hammer. This will produce a dent. Experiment on scraps first. You will find it is possible to create various types of scars. A genuine dent or scar is seldom uniform in depth. Try to achieve the haphazard variations of depth and direction made by excessive wear.

SCRATCHES AND ROUGHENING

A stiff wire brush of the type used to remove paint for refinishing is a handy tool for roughwork. Maintain an even pressure when scratching the wood's surface. Scratches that go with the grain are done with light pressure; work done against the grain requires a firmer stroke.

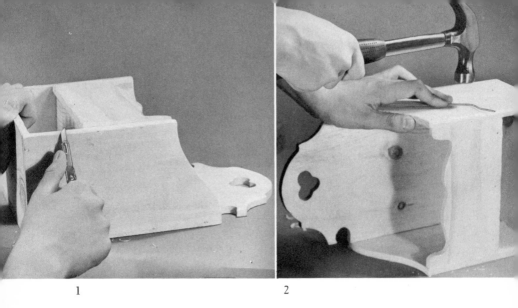

1. Knife is used to nick and scratch new candlebox holder and to soften edges for antique effect. 2. Worm tracings are simulated by hammering a piece of bent wire on surface. 3. Additional aging of wood is accomplished with a blowtorch, lightly used. Avoid excessive

A HUNDRED YEARS WITH A BLAST OF HEAT

You can age wood in a few moments with a blowtorch. This makes it dark and imparts a delightful form of rough-and-ready patina that can later add subtle tonal values when staining is applied. Employ safeguards when handling a blowtorch; this is no toy for children. Work in a well-ventilated, open area—away from fumes or oil-soaked rags. Make several tryouts before turning the torch against your working object's surface. Wood scraps will do nicely. Study the effects of various distances and times. Use a medium flame and play it lightly and rapidly over the wood. Don't stay in one part more than a moment or it may catch fire. An occasional burn is interesting, but large seared areas are too obvious and look phony. After scorching the surface, use a small wire brush or putty knife lightly to scrape away the charred material.

CHAINS ARE HANDY TOO

In the pseudo-antique business, a favorite tool of the fakers is a length of heavy chain. Swinging enthusiastically, these antique charlatans can make a footstool from the corner hardware store look old enough to hail from Louis XIV's milking barns. The trick is a good one. The size of the links should be scaled according to the size of the working piece. Generally, small pieces call for small links. Large pieces can use small or large links, or both. Do your flailing in the open, or in a workshop with a high ceiling. Don't overexert yourself; light blows are sufficient. (Heavier ones

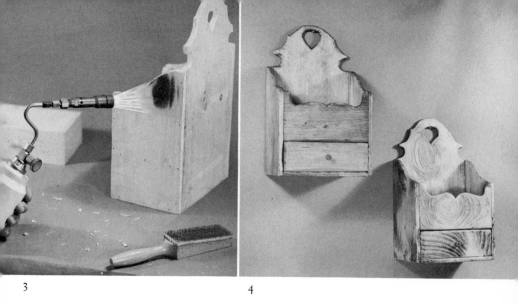

burning. A rough steel brush is another handy antiquing tool. 4. The newly finished antique *(left)* is not easily distinguished from the 150-year-old example at right as they hang side by side on a wall. *(Courtesy Martin Ennimigazi)*

could break the piece to bits.) Two or three blows are enough. The chain length should be about twenty-four inches. (See page 186.)

FINISHING TECHNIQUES

Now that you've done a good job of distressing the surface of your antiqued object, it's time to do the real job. Lightly sand the surface with 4/o or 6/o sandpaper. Then apply a stain. There are dozens of available stains which will suggest mahogany, cherry, fruitwood, oak, pine, walnut, or any other tree that grows. Select a stain that is valid for the piece to be finished. If a Colonial table of a certain style was originally created in Vermont, for example, select a stain that indicates a wood native to Vermont.

When using any stain, it is best to thin it, rather than use it full strength from the container. You can then apply several light coats, instead of just one heavy coat. This allows a gradual building up of color until the desired intensity is reached.

In staining, too, there are small tricks which produce dramatic results. Here are a few.

Rub the raw wood down with rottenstone or pumice mixed with water. This adds highlights to the previously sanded wood grain. It is necessary to wash the surface with a stiff brush and water after the rubbing. Let it stand for twenty-four hours, then sand it once more. You can then apply your staining finish.

Chairs and other new furniture can be weathered by blows with a chain for antique look.

Grain filler adds highlights to the grain of the wood. It is normally used on open-grain woods, but try it on any wood commonly associated with Colonial antiques. Brush the filler on against the grain, using a scrubbing brush. Exert moderate pressure. Wipe the surface smooth with a clean cloth, working in the direction of the grain to remove excess filler.

Two or three applications are possible to build up the desired effect. Do your prior testing on scrap wood of the same variety and note the results, then decide on the number of applications necessary to produce the result you want.

Motor oil adds age to certain wood surfaces. Apply some with a rag after the first coat of finish has been applied. Twist the rag hard against the surface to force oil into the grain of the wood. Confine this technique to small areas, thus avoiding a uniform darkness rather than the haphazard tones which are your goal. This oil toning is particularly effective in areas close to knots; the darkened area draws the viewer's eye away from unsightly knots or blemishes.

Shoe polish, particularly the oil-stain type, sometimes makes a good final coat. When this is applied over several coats of stain, it is possible to use a shoe brush to buff up luster in the wood. A buffing wheel, used lightly, produces a rich sheen and depth to the finish.

Paste wax and steel wool make an alternative method of final finishing. Repeated light coats of paste wax, buffed and rubbed down with the wool, create a finish of depth. After the final wool rubbing, use a slightly dampened lamb's-wool bonnet (the kind associated with buffing on an electric drill) and hand-rub the surfaces. This produces a mellow patina.

These, then, are professional wood-finishing methods which can lift your antiquing project high out of the ordinary and make your workshop sessions pure delight.

New Life for Old Junk

If you can't even draw a straight line, consider yourself fortunate. Crooked lines are much more interesting. The well-known gentleman named Peter Hunt has made a career out of crooked lines—freehand lines, to be more specific. Using some simple carpentry tools, paint, and discarded junk from attics and bargain basements, he has instigated a system for bringing discards back to life, which he calls "Transformagic."

Do you enjoy the quaint cheerfulness of Pennsylvania-German decoration? Why pay large sums for somebody else's imitation? Create your own interpretations of this truly American folk art.

A battered bench table *(left)* made of uninterestingly textured wood became a gay picnic table *(below)* when painted by Peter Hunt. *(Photos courtesy DuPont)*

What do you need? An assortment of bright enamel paints, some brushes, turpentine, and rags. What do you work on? Old furniture, discarded packing boxes, five-and-dime-store trays, coffeepots, picture frames—anything old that you want to make new.

An old wheelbarrow was transformed by Peter Hunt into the attractive
food wagon. Designs can be painted freehand or they can be stenciled.
(*Photos courtesy DuPont*)

See things through new eyes. Imagine that old chifforobe, for example,
with its knobby legs sawed off, the rococo scrollwork chiseled away, and
all the scarred paint deleted with sandpaper and paint remover. Reduce
the item to basic simplicity. Cover it with a coat of white or colored
primer, and then let your imagination take over.

How do you start? A good beginning might be to draw a deliberately
irregular line of bright color across the edges, creating a sort of frame
within which to decorate. Repeat this motif around all other edges. Don't
labor over this; the charm of the technique lies in its honest simplicity.

You can create serpentine lines by joining together short, curved strokes.
Plump little hearts can be repeated at intervals above and below the
boundaries for variety. Other Pennsylvania-German trademarks are scrollwork, flowers, grasses of many hues, barnyard animals in stylized simplicity,
leaves, vegetables, and hex symbols (adapted from geometric figures which
can still be found on many Pennsylvania barns, whose original purpose,
according to popular legend, was to drive away evil spirits, but which more
probably were just decorations).

Plan your over-all design on paper first. This will enable you to visualize the completed sections in color, seeing how they harmonize and carry
out the theme. Authentic motifs can be found in many books.

TIPS ON TECHNIQUE

Keep the background *in the background*. Work large. This eliminates
any tendency toward tightness, and makes your motifs visible from a distance. Make your designs bright and your background hue neutral. Use a
water-color brush for small details, adding these touches after the enamel-
painted larger areas have dried. The water color can be made durable by
lacquering on top afterward.

Want to impart an antique finish? After the background and detail painting has dried, cover the entire object with liquid glaze. When glazing large items, wipe away excess glaze with a circular motion by wiping toward the edges from the center. Do one half of the work at a time to avoid the glaze from becoming tacky before you are ready for the second half.

Antiquing a tray. A glaze of oil color is applied over tray. Antique effect is begun by wiping glaze from tray in light, circular motion with soft cloth—working from center toward edges. In third photo, center is almost glaze free. Blending is completed by patting tray with edge of a dry paint brush.

The antiquing effect is amplified by wiping with hardest pressure in the center, then lightening pressure as you work toward the edges. The wiping is actually a blending process and is done with clean cheesecloth. In addition to wiping with a circular motion, do a bit of patting in the same manner. Then, finally, take a large clean house-painting brush and

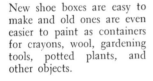

New shoe boxes are easy to make and old ones are even easier to paint as containers for crayons, wool, gardening tools, potted plants, and other objects.

repeat the same motions with this. Pat the hairs of the brush lightly against the work. The glaze will thus pick up a slightly mottled, ancient appearance. It may be diluted with turpentine if too dark, and it may be kept moist with a few drops of linseed oil if you are a slow worker.

GLOSSING

Use high-gloss paints for lightly decorated areas and flat paints for backgrounds. If working on new wood, use an undercoat first to help size it. Follow this same procedure if working over dark, original colors with new, lighter color. If the original area was too dark, sand it away and start anew. Satiny, semigloss paints are made by adding some flat, undercoat paint to the high-gloss enamel. Since undercoat paint is usually white, this not only will satinize the sheen of the paint but will also lighten its hue.

If you plan to combine high glossing with antiquing, just remember to apply the glazing after the paint is dry to the touch, then wipe away any glaze from areas you wish to be highlighted. The bright paint will glow through in contrast to the more subdued hues where it is covered with glaze. Any puddles of glaze on carved work can be absorbed with a rag or dry brush. Avoid puddling; it makes the finished work look amateur.

Proper method for applying colors

Work with only one color at a time and let it dry. This means to paint in all parts of a design bearing one color before proceeding to the use of the next one. The simplest palette for Pennsylvania-German art is the four colors most commonly used by the pioneering farmers—red, blue, yellow, and green. By adding white to these you can come up with a fine assortment of hues. It is not a good idea to mix colors—yellow with blue, for example, to produce a third color, green. The results are often haphazard, and the exact shades will certainly be hard to duplicate for matching.

Suitability of motifs

Finally, we come to the matter of purpose. A decorated piece must be at home in the room for which it is intended. Do not use vegetable motifs in a playroom. They look better in the kitchen or dining area. Mate the design to the function of the area.

Special effects

You can duplicate the appearance of marble quite easily. Marbleizing is done in the following manner:

Use a red sable brush (water-color type) with a three-fourth-inch width, a fairly large-bristled oil-color brush measuring about two or three inches in width, and a feather like a goose quill, or gull feather. First, give the working surface two coats of paint, using the color which suggests the marble you have in mind. While the second coat is wet, dip your sable brush in the contrasting color which will be the marbleized effect, sweep it loosely across the background color in long, waving strokes, and then quickly merge it into the background with the wide bristle brush, swept dry over the work. Next, dip the feather tip in a second color of paint and draw the tip (not the quill) across the broader veins you have just put on with the sable brush. Again, quickly sweep across this with the dry bristle brush. Allow to dry and the marbleizing is done.

Suggested marbleizing colors are: pink background with black and white veining, or black background with white and green veining.

Marbleizing is appropriate for garden furniture, table tops, and wooden furniture with wrought-iron legs. Don't concern yourself too literally with matching true marble; the effect is more pleasing if you strive for an obviously painted appearance. Old Victorian furniture and severe modern look equally interesting when marbleized. For contrast, you might paint in an edging of dull black leaves with a maple or ivy motif. If furniture is to be used outside or on a screened porch where it will be subject to weathering, it is a good idea to apply three or four coats of spar varnish over the marbleizing.

Shadow boxes and hanging shelves

Take old picture frames—the heavier and more elaborately carved the better—and turn them into useful, decorative objects. Just tack on a plywood backing, paint in white with an application of glazing to antique it, and hang on the wall. Shelves may be added to hold small plants, vases, glass bottles, and similar bric-a-brac. The same picture frame with a solid backing, laid flat on painted sawhorse legs, becomes a handy coffee table. Don't bother to nail the frame to the legs—if the legs are hinged to fold up, the entire serving table can be stored out of sight when desirable. The picture-frame serving tray is thus also removable for taking out to the kitchen or carrying from guest to guest. Be sure to lacquer the frame and legs to protect them from spilled foods and liquids.

Courtesy DuPont

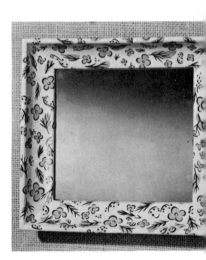

Courtesy American Crayon

Old picture frames can be made into shadow boxes with easily constructed shelving *(left)*. Newly painted and with simple designs, picture frames can also house a new mirror, as shown above.

20

Creative Jewelry

Anybody, really anybody, can create unusual, good-looking jewelry. You need no experience, just common-sense technical skill to start the project. Half an hour, and you can complete your first project.

What You Need to Start

One pair of jeweler's pliers with combined side-cutters is the only necessary tool. You will find these pliers invaluable for all-around hobby work as well as jewelry crafts. The nose of the pliers comes to a point, making it easy to twist wire and make loops. Smooth jaws do not mar the metal. The side cutters, far back on the jaws, are used to snip off excess wire. Another pair of pliers, although not necessary, sometimes proves helpful in making tight twists. Suggested is a small, flat-nosed pliers. With this in one hand and the jeweler's pliers in the other, the work can be held firm while the twists are made. The pliers are shown in the accompanying photographs.

The basic material from which you design any number of earrings, pendants, pins, and cuff links is soft-annealed, 20-gauge silver wire. Various other materials may be used to express your taste and ingenuity. They might be semiprecious stones, rare natural materials, and even small curiosities. Don't feel, however, that your projects are limited to these materials only. Attractive shells picked up at the bench, odd or colorful pebbles, provocative old buttons and any other small and durable object you like can be set in jewelry.

Earrings in a Moment or Two

Just about any stone, bead, or object that has a center hole, or that can be drilled, can become an earring almost instantly. Take a short length of silver wire, bend a tiny loop at the bottom, and crimp it tight with the nose of your pliers. This makes a small knob to prevent your stone from slipping off the wire. Now slide your stone onto the wire, make a loop near the top, and then wind the wire around itself in a tight, regular spiral. Cut off excess wire and squeeze the end inconspicuously into your design.

If the spiral is too loose, this can be remedied by judicious use of the pliers. If it just doesn't go right the first time, unwind the wire and start over again; nothing will be lost. With practice you will become surprisingly accurate.

Now you have a pendant stone that can be hung on a silver earring attachment known as a "finding" and stocked by jewelry supply stores. This earring-back has a decorative dome, and a sturdy little link for attaching your pendant stone. The link opens and closes with a twist of pliers. A simple, but attractive, attachment for pierced ears can be made of the basic 20-gauge silver wire. But be sure to smooth the end of the wire with emery cloth or a fine file.

Bracelets, Necklaces, and Other Jewelry

To make bracelets or necklaces with a dangling effect, loop your pendant stones through the links of a chain, a spaced distance apart. Then wrap your tight spirals as before. A heavy, decorative silver chain may be used, or a lighter, simple sterling chain. The silver clasp is easily attached with pliers. Using the same principle, stones may be wired with a loop at either side and connected in sequence to form another type of bracelet or necklace. Each small variation in the technique produces a new group of possibilities. To make cuff links, simply connect two of your little units. Semiprecious stones are suggested. These cost relatively little while looking expensive.

Unusual Ideas

Quite often you will find curious or evocative objects ready-made, if only you could figure out how to use them. Your wire-working method is usually adaptable. Early American shoe buttons, for instance, make unique jewelry. Made of rich black brass, with a bright center knob and strong loop behind for fastening, they are excellent examples of the everyday craftsmanship of an older time. They can be strung together in the way we have been discussing, to form a heavy key chain or neck chain. Hanging several short strands on earring attachments would be effective.

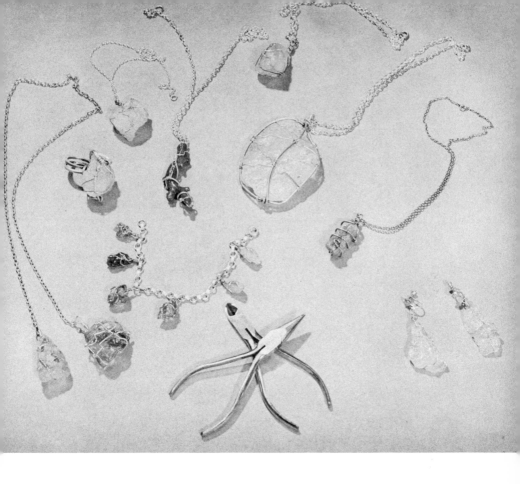

Attractive jewelry made by the gem-caging process. At left, wrap-around tie pendant with aquamarine and amethyst. Other items include caged ring with rose quartz and caged pendants with rose quartz, amethyst, topaz, and raw gem coral. All pieces were made without soldering and without any tools other than the two pairs of pliers shown in the picture. (*Courtesy Sam Kramer*)

By using heavier 10-gauge wire along with your lighter wire, the horizons are again enlarged. Now you can make hairpins with several turquoise nuggets grouped loosely at the top, or with a branch of deep red gem coral jutting from the hair. (Most of these semiprecious stones cost between twenty-five cents and three dollars each.) If the heavier wire is hammered somewhat after it is bent and twisted into the required shapes, it assumes a textured and forged look that gives the work a more authoritative flavor.

A household claw hammer may be used for pounding. Use the flat face and it will make subtle, irregular planes on the wire, flattening it and changing its contour at the same time. The first few hammer blows will tell you the amount of force you should use to get the most effective surface. You may want to use the round end of the hammer; that's up to you, and you will soon discover what interesting effects are possible with a bit of experimentation.

Why not make free-form shapes of the heavier wire and attach mobile or fixed parts to form pendants or pins? Although much stronger, the heavier-gauge wire is still extremely simple to loop and twist. When making a pin, a length of the 12-gauge wire is allowed to extend, and then bent backward to catch in a small hook fashioned from the same material. The pin mechanism is then an integral part of the whole design, and functions very much like an ordinary safety pin. In order to work properly, however, the pin end should be filed or hammered to a point.

Making Rings

Simply spiral the heavy wire into two or three close circlets large enough to fit the finger. Start by twisting the small mooring loop at the top and finish by winding the end of your wire onto the base of this same little loop. It makes an unexpectedly stout ring, and you can attach decorative or amusing things: a couple of flopping stones, for example, or a mass of beads or antique buttons, piled and domed to give an oriental feeling. Band rings are made by splicing two or more finger-sized spirals of heavy wire together with the light-gauge wire. This splicing technique will lend itself to other ring uses, chain making, bracelet and necklace catches. It can be employed in countless ways.

Cementing Techniques

Now, suppose you are at the seashore and find a small piece of driftwood, a fantastic shell, or fragment of curious bottle glass sculptured by the waves. You see these things as pieces of jewelry, yet there are no holes for securing them. What to do? First, let's not overlook the function of cementing. Anything imaginable can be transformed into a piece of jewelry by cementing the proper attachments to the back. A preassembled pin-back, for example, complete with safety catch, transforms any object into a wearable brooch. This finding is priced around fifteen cents. Antique buttons, coins, and shells can be cemented to sterling earring backs which have a shallow cup for the purpose. Most semiprecious stones also respond to the cementing method. Cemented pieces should not be used for rings, since they are subject to too much wear and buffeting, but are quite safe and permanent in other kinds of jewelry.

There are a few elementary precautions to take to insure firm cementing work. Use Duco or some other good household cement, and make sure the object is clean and dry and free from oil or grease. Don't be afraid to use plenty of cement, and, most important of all, let it dry rock-hard before touching it. Most people who cement things impatiently test them in an hour and spoil the bond.

"Caging a Gem"

Instead of cementing, these same irregular objects can be used by wrapping or binding them in silver wire. The art of caging or netting gems is merely an extension of the wire work already discussed, except now you are dealing with stones and objects that have no holes, and hence must be literally tied in little bundles, using the soft wire in place of twine. The method is easy, and the effect is charming. Irregular, glittering, uncut stones raw from the earth lend themselves best to this work. Smaller pieces are excellent for matching earrings, cuff links or rings. Crystalline chunks of honey-colored citrine or grape-purple amethyst make rich brace-let settings, huge rings, or smaller neck ornaments and brooches. Aqua-marine, a stone with a mysterious under-water quality, is expensive in appearance but a good sample costs only five dollars.

How to prepare caged stones

To begin, study the stone, turning it to decide which end will be the top. Select the most interesting side for the face. Usually the more dimensional side is best for the front, the flatter side best for the back. Take advantage of the irregularities of the stone for mooring your wire. Using your fingers and pliers, bind the malleable wire in a simple criss-cross, exactly as though tying a tiny package. At the places where the wires cross, wrap one around the other once or twice for security, just as you do with string. Now twist a loop at the top, and you have an earring or bracelet pendant, or, with a larger stone, a neck pendant. There are practically no rules to this game; rather, you invent your own rules. You can start with one strand of wire, or several, and you may introduce new wires any time you need them. Just moor the extra piece with a few wraps around an already fixed wire, draw it across the stone, and moor it to another strand. Continue weaving and binding, mooring and looping, crisscrossing back and forth, from side to side and from front to back. Keep in mind that, though the stone must be held securely, it is not esthetically pleasing to have too many wires cutting across its surfaces. If the stone feels loose in its wire basket, tighten it by giving the wire short, zigzag bends or kinks with the tip ends of the pliers.

When working with larger pieces, 12-gauge (heavier) wire can once again be introduced. Use it as a frame around the object, with the lighter wires moored to it and crisscrossing back and forth. Or make the weightier wire snake across the front of the stone with the thinner wire weaving around from front to back.

A stone with several natural clefts and projections may be held with a minimum of wire, while a smoother stone with less acute forms might require a good deal more "caging" to hold it securely. A long, narrow stone would require a different treatment from a shorter, more massive stone, and so on. However, even cabochon (flat) stones can be caged and held securely by taking the proper precautions, front and back. By means of binding and wrapping, almost any caged piece can also be secured to an attachment or finding, particularly one-piece pin backs or cuff-link backs. Sometimes, several stones will be used in a single piece, separately for contrast of color and form, or wired and worked together as a single unit to achieve strange and rich effects. Other times you will seek a severe, almost classical result. Caged pendant stones can be hung on a leather throng or a colored ribbon. Jewels, netted in silver, can be strung like precious charms on a bracelet or necklace of larger-linked chain. Fobs and chatelaines can also be developed with lengths of chain and caged gems. All the methods described earlier for pierced stones can be modified for use with the caging technique.

Making a Silver Snowflake for Christmas

Here is a project in creating a stylized snowflake pendant which you cannot currently buy at any price. The same basic techniques are adaptable to the fashioning of a Christmas tree, sunburst, starfish—virtually any literal or abstract shape. See illustrations on pages 200-201.

Pieces like this make intriguing gifts and, like any well-designed handcraft item, can be sold for profit. The resulting jewelry is both practical and unique.

The entire outlay in equipment consists of a jeweler's saw frame and pliers, plus a semiprecious stone, a sheet of sterling silver, and a silver chain on which to hang the snowflake. Sawblades are inexpensive, a matter of a few cents each, and, correctly used, they will last a long time.

Silver is recommended because it is a precious metal, moderate in cost and most responsive to sawing. But you can substitute any other metal, if you wish, from tin to platinum.

An amethyst was selected for the heart of the snowflake shown in the step-by-step photograph. The deep purple of this stone makes a brilliant contrast against silver. It, too, is relatively low in cost, considering the quality it imparts to the pendant. The whole kit—saw, pliers, sawblades, silver sheet and chain, and the stone—can be purchased for around eleven or twelve dollars. The tools are a worthwhile investment for repeated use through the years.

[198]

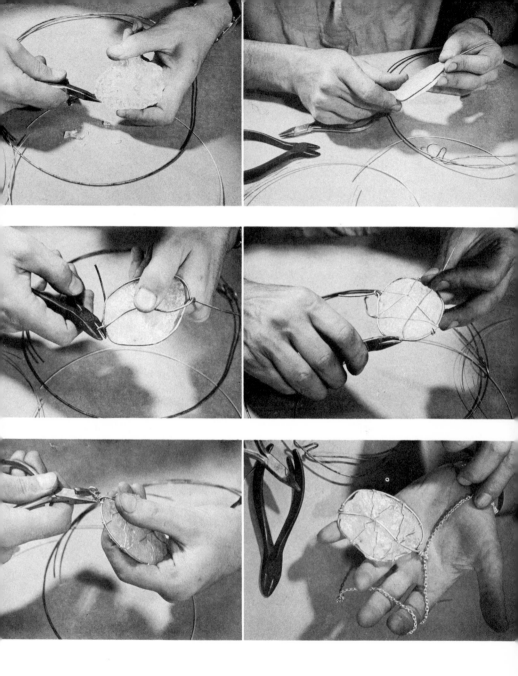

Five steps in caging the gem shown at bottom right used as a pendant. Ragged bits are chipped off with pliers and grooves are made for silver wire to secure the stone as shown in the second photo. The anchoring continues with another heavy piece of wire twisted to hold at back, and thinner gauge wire interlaced over the front. A looped coil is made from the protruding wire at top. Note kinks in wire made with pliers for decorative effect and to tighten wire over stone.

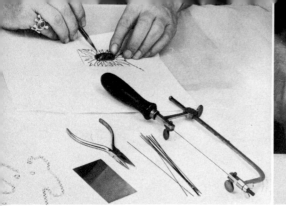

Making a silver snowflake pendant. A sheet of silver (2 inches x 3 inches) is placed on paper. Trace around edges, then position stone (amethyst) in center and draw shapes suggesting rays all around it. Four narrow sections are left between rays. These will be bent up to hold the stone. Allow for enough metal at top to bend into holder for chain. Cut out tracing and paste on sheet of silver. Cut through paper and silver

Sawing, the basis of this project, is among the easiest of jeweler's techniques to master. Practice will make you fast and certain in your control. A few tips: always insert a blade into the saw frame with its teeth pointed down. Saw with an up-and-down movement, not horizontally as with a carpenter's tool. Remember, since the teeth point down, all cutting is done on the downstroke only. Do not use too much pressure when sawing. Let it glide along practically of its own volition, as you follow the outlines of your sketch. If a sawblade breaks, don't be upset. They're expendable.

The wingnut at the top of the saw frame should be loosened before inserting a new blade, then gradually tightened when the blade is secured. Twang the blade with your finger to check tightness. It should ring out with a high note. A tight blade is an accurate one.

Always start a cut with a small upstroke. This makes a groove to steady your downstroke. Saw with long, easy strokes until you come to a corner or tight turn, then use short, light strokes. If you break a blade and a good-sized piece remains, don't throw it away; just adjust the saw frame to a shorter span, and you're back in business.

The steps in making the snowflake pendant are described under the accompanying illustrations. A final point: when you are cutting out the prongs which will clamp the stone in place within the snowflake, work carefully. You want that amethyst to fit in securely and not fall out while it is being worn. Silver is soft and can be bent about easily to your desire.

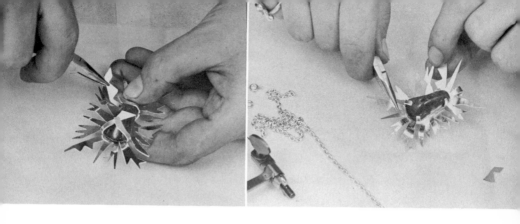

together. Wash off paper design, position amethyst, and bend up the four sections into prongs to hold stone at edges. Trim away excess prong lengths with saw. Twist silver gently so metal won't break or tear. Roughness on sawed edges can be smoothed with emery cloth. Add a silver chain through the twisted loop at top. Price of materials is less than one-fourth what the piece would cost in a store.

When you have made your first snowflake design, you may have found it so delightful a project that you will decide to create many more for personalized Christmas giving. Bear in mind that the same simple procedures can be reapplied to fashion other free-form shapes. Thus, regardless of the occasion or season, you can create an appropriate symbol in precious metal and gems.

The finished pendant.

Source of Supplies

The tools and supplies used for these projects were obtained from the Studio of Sam Kramer, noted designer. He will send interested readers a full catalogue of information and findings upon request. Write to Mr. Kramer at 29 West 8 Street, New York 11, N.Y.

Some Semiprecious Gems and Their Characteristics

Turquoise. Blue-green, irregular shape, often with matrix patterns running through gem. Priced from around $1.00 for smaller stones to $2.00 for larger ones.

Onyx. Greenish-black to grass-green color. Around $1.50 per gem.

Carnelian. A russet-orange hue, usually bead-shaped. Costs around $1.00 per stone or less.

Quartz. Hardest of the semiprecious stones; comes in pink, rose, and ice-clear colors. Average cost is around $1.50 for large pendant stones.

Malachite. A greenish stone, often available in the form of beads for somewhere around sixty to seventy cents per dozen.

Coral. An organic by-product from the sea, available in many colors, including white, pink, yellow, red, blue. A red gem coral costs around $3.00.

Amethyst. Various intensities of deep lavender to grape purple; costs from $2.50 to $3.00 per gem on an average.

Citrine. Oddly shaped chunks of honey-colored crystal. Price from $2.00 to $3.00 per gem.

Aquamarine. A shimmering water-blue stone, prized for its clarity and costing from about $5.00 up, depending on color and carat size.

We have discussed the caged-gem procedure because of its unusual nature, but the possibilities in jewelcraft are virtually endless and, in most cases, require few tools beyond pliers, cement, rouge, and polishing accessories, as long as you work with the rough stones. Gem cutting, of course, requires more elaborate equipment and is thus beyond the intended scope of this book.

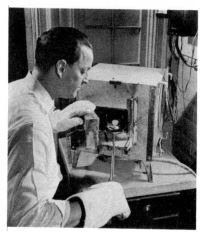

Edward Winter working at his kiln.

21

Enameling on Metal

Nobody knows for certain when the art of enameling was discovered. Historians place its origin at least as far back as ancient Egypt and fifth-century B.C. China. Other countries may also lay claim to the art; the fact remains that it was practiced long before the Christian era came into being.

Today, enameling is one of America's leading hobbycrafts, and a number of modestly priced kits are available. These are quite satisfactory for introductory projects, having furnaces which will accept work up to about three inches in diameter. This size is suitable for the making of earrings, tie pins, small ash trays, costume jewelry, and buttons. The serious enamelist will certainly want to progress beyond these beginnings, and for that purpose we have included in this chapter an illustrated section describing the steps for making your own enameling furnace for an outlay of ten dollars or so. You may purchase furnaces of larger sizes for around thirty or thirty-five dollars and upward.

Though enameling is a professional business, its part-time devotees include homemakers, casual artists, educators, occupational-therapy patients, and even children. Because the process requires extremely high temperatures, any work done by young people should be properly supervised, and safety precautions stressed.

Enameling can be a gay deceiver the first time around. It looks so easy to do! Just drop the powdered frit onto the metal, and when it is fired it runs, blobs, and streaks so provocatively! The results are exciting and unpredictable. The neophyte clasps his hands in glee. Aren't the results unique? And that, then, is the danger; uniqueness becomes the permanent excuse for uncontrollability. The tyro enamelist cannot repeat what he has done, nor can he retain any information for future projects. Learning your craft is a requisite for intelligent enameling.

What *is* enameling? It is the fusing of glass to metal by the application of heat. The glass comes in the form of commercially prepared powders, ground to 80-mesh fineness. When they are fused, they produce specific colors. A properly enameled piece is durable; it will last for thousands of years, and its colors will remain unchanged.

Tools for the enameling craft are not numerous. The main one is the furnace—never call it a kiln in this field—and it operates at temperatures near 1500° F. In an emergency you can use a blowtorch in place of the furnace, helped along by a hand bellows to raise its temperature.

The Basics in Enameling

A few metal-working tools will prove valuable, for even a hobbyist should cut out his own metal shapes and then form them over a pounding stake. A heavy tree stump or log cut straight across to make a flat working top is excellent for use in pounding and shaping. (You can also make heavy metal dies in the shape of an ash tray or bowl, then lay your metal over the die and pound the object into the desired shape.) Pounding should be done with ball-peen hammers or mallets. Metal cutting is done with tinning shears and any form of metal-working saw.

Your first experiment will be a revelation. You will probably over-decorate, but when the powdered colors have been applied through a sieve over a base of gum tragacanth and then inserted into the furnace, you will stand by impatiently, waiting for the enamels to fuse and take on their characteristic hues. The firing is done at 1450° to 1500° F. and usually takes only a few minutes. Then the piece is carefully removed from the furnace with tongs and placed on a sheet of asbestos board to cool. Examine this first try critically. Do not be satisfied simply to produce a colorful, garish piece. Enameling has an incredible range of subtleties. You can fire the piece again, adding a second color design. Always bear in mind that enameling is not a hit-and-miss procedure. It can be controlled, and that is the great challenge.

Enamels designed by Kenneth Bates. (*Courtesy Cleveland Museum of Art*)

A Brief History of Enameling

The first true enameling technique historically recorded is known as "champlevé" and was probably invented, or at least perfected, by ancient Egyptian craftsmen. It is a method by which metal is gouged out of an object and the voided space then filled with colorful enamels. The Chinese went a step further by inventing cloisonnée—the use of wire to separate and contain variously hued enamels. Skillfully produced cloisonnée bowls are prized items in our museums. An authentic Chinese cloisonnée may be worth thousands of dollars, or even be priceless. This early technique was adapted in a sense by the French craftsmen of medieval Europe who *painted* the same effects with enamels. Another variation of the cloisonnée technique involves no use of wire dividers, but simply consists of taking the fired enamel piece while it is still in molten form and plunging it into a tank of water. This shatters the enamel and it hardens with tiny cracks throughout.

Getting Started in Enameling

Enamels come in a wide assortment of colors available at moderate cost. Usually, transparent enamels fuse at somewhat lower temperature than opaques. The firing temperatures are specified by the manufacturers of the products.

We shall not go into detail about this subject, for enameling is so versatile a medium that its many avenues of exploration would—and do— fill lengthy books. Our recommendation is that you make your first attempts using a hobbycraft kit, then graduate to making your own furnace or purchasing (possibly secondhand) a larger one which will enable you to make large bowls, plaques, and inserts for such items as book ends, address plates, lamp bases, boxes, and similar objects.

The best metal for enameling is copper because of its moderate cost, beautiful luster, and pliability when shaping. Enameling may also be done on silver and aluminum, as these metals also can be worked, hammered, and polished to emphasize the play of light and internal reflection through transparent enamels.

A few words about preparing your metal for enameling. It must be spotlessly clean. Prepare a cleaning solution by adding one part of sulphuric or nitric acid to five parts of water (acid into water—never the reverse!). Always wear rubber gloves when working with acid. Immerse the metal in this solution for about ten minutes, then rinse it off under running water. Do not touch the surface with your bare fingers, since the slightest touch of grease or perspiration will make the adhering of enamel difficult. Dry the metal with sawdust. (Keep a box of sawdust handy for the purpose and drop the object into it, then pour more on top.) Lift out the metal with tongs. The reason for preferring sawdust to ordinary air drying is that metal left in the air to dry may oxidize, causing some loss of quality to the finished piece, particularly if transparent enamels are being applied.

Some Tips on Applying the Enamel

Beginners will find it desirable to apply a flux (clear, colorless enamel) over the metal before using colored enamels. Put on the flux and fire the piece until it fuses to a hard, glassy coating. You may then sprinkle your colored enamels on the cool piece, applying it either through a wire mesh or a pepper shaker. The subsequent firing will fuse the enamel frit onto the surface. A large camel's-hair brush is also useful for first wetting the metal surface so that the powder will stick. Or you may use the gum tragacanth solution for this same purpose. (A simple substitute is to boil a few flakes of gum agar in water and let it jell for a couple of hours, after which it may be picked up with your brush, dipped into water slightly, and then painted over the metal surface.) Designs are applied to the work through a stencil, or by pushing the enamel powder about with a water-moistened or dry camel's-hair brush.

Set the enamel-sprinkled object aside until the water evaporates. (You can rest it in your kitchen oven for several minutes at about 200°-250° F. to speed up the drying.) Once it is dry, it may be put in the furnace and fired.

Enameling is properly done on both sides of a rounded piece. This is known as counter-enameling. It prevents the enamels from flaking off and improves the final appearance. The counter-enameling is done after the inside surface of concave objects or the top of flat pieces has been enameled and completed. Turn the object upside down on a nickel screen or on a twisted wire tripod and then follow the original procedure once more.

What can you do with your finished enamels? They make wonderful personalized gifts, will brighten up your home, and can be put to many utilitarian purposes. You can sell your work too, but this is a field best left to the professional who knows merchandising and can produce in large volume. The profit to a hobby-enamelist exists in the sense of having produced useful, well-designed artifacts which will be treasured by the recipients for many years to come.

Enamel brooch in a simple fish design made by Audrey Nelson.

How to build an enamel furnace at a cost of around ten dollars.

1. To construct kiln, mark dimensions with pencil on fireblock. Use flat stick as a guide. Cut fireblock with handsaw and save the scrap pieces.

2. After pieces are cut, lay out location of channels to hold heating element. Using a straight edge, scrape channels into fireblock with screwdriver or chisel. Do not dig channels to full depth yet.

3. Cut angular slope for door opening with a heavy rasp, and use one of scrap pieces to form back of kiln.

4. When pieces have been cut and prepared to this point, fit together by rubbing one against another to make tight joint.

5. Remove top block and fit heating elements. Now scrape channels deeper, if necessary, to make snug fit. Assemble blocks and heating elements so end wires protrude at back.

6. Use 1-inch-x-1-inch angle irons to hold furnace walls together, and use four metal strips to encircle and reinforce kiln. Bend ends and drill a ¼-inch hole. Tie together so ends fasten tightly with bolts, washers, and nuts.

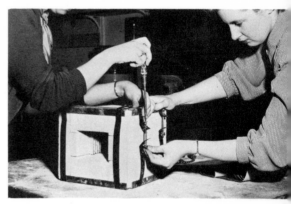

7. Connect electric cord to ends of heating element. Use remaining scrap to make door with two bolts. Fill least half an inch from face of kiln. Make handle out of heavy wire. Attach handle and asbestos sheet to door with two bolts. Fill countersunk bolt holes with saliminite cement. Also smear cement on sides of door and opening to prevent excessive wear. Do not cement joints of fireblock. Use a trowel to load kiln and place enamel on a stainless steel bridge, never on floor of kiln.

8. Enameled plaque (made by a student of John Adams High School, Cleveland) is cemented to center of wooden box.

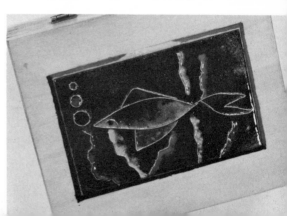

Where to Obtain Enameling Supplies

Enamels.
B. F. Drakenfield & Co., 45 Park Place, New York 7, N.Y.
Thomas C. Thompson, 1205 Deerfield Rd., Highland Park, Ill.
John T. King Co., 147 Chestnut St., Providence, R.I.
Maas and Waldstein Co., 440 Riverside Ave., Newark 4, N.J.
Zapon Co., Stamford, Conn.

Metals.
COPPER
Revere Copper and Brass Co., 230 Park Ave., New York, N.Y.
GUILDERS' METAL
Chase Brass and Copper Company. Any city (address in phone book)
T. E. Conklin Co., 54 Lafayette St., New York 13, N.Y.
STEEL
American Rolling Mills, or Republic Steel Company (both with warehouses and stock in all cities). Ask for a special steel called enameling stock (16- or 18-gauge)
SILVER AND GOLD
Eastern Smelting and Refining Corp., 107 West Brookline, Boston.
Handy and Harmon, 82 Fulton St., New York 7, N.Y.
Goldsmith Bros. Smelting Co., 58 East Washington St., Chicago, Ill.
I. Miller, Inc., 304 Colonial Arcade, Cleveland, Ohio

Tools.
William Dixon, Inc., 32 East Kinney St., Newark 2, N.J.
Patterson Bros., 15 Park Row, New York 7, N.Y.
Metal Crafts Supply Co., Providence, R.I.
Norton Co., Worcester, Mass.
Newall Mfg. Co., 29 East Madison St., Chicago, Ill.

Tanks and Torches.
The Prest-O-Lite Co., 30 East 42 St., New York 17, N.Y.

Enameling Furnaces (Laboratory and Box Muffle Type).
Ferro Enamel Corp., 4150 East 56 St., Cleveland, Ohio
Hevi Duty Electric Co., Milwaukee 1, Wis.
Hoskins Furnace Co., Detroit, Mich.
Harrop Ceramic Service Co., 35 East Gay St., Columbus, Ohio
Pereny Equipment Co., 893 Chambers Rd., Columbus, Ohio

Jewel Findings, Pins, etc.
Sam Kramer, 29 West 8 St., New York 11, N.Y.
Metal Findings Corp., 150 West 22 St. New York 11, N.Y.

Protective Asbestos Gloves.
Des Moines Glove & Mfg. Co., Des Moines, Iowa

22
_____

Glass Decorating

Stained Glass

A N ACCIDENT made by a long-forgotten potter may have provided the origin of stained glass. Fragments of pottery many thousands of years old have been unearthed, and some bear the unmistakable touch of glazing. From the fusing of sand and soda to the surface of a ceramic piece that may have fallen into a fire came our discovery of glass for decorative purposes. And in time, this beautiful, versatile medium graduated to the making of inlays which might reflect and coruscate the rays of the sun.

As the centuries unfolded, craftsmen learned how to add chemicals to the molten glass, producing a wide array of colors. And finally, a few centuries before Christ, the Roman artisans fashioned colored glass for windows. It was a costly medium, and crude. The first glass panes were cast on stone, and this rough surface produced sheets of colored glass which could transmit light, but afforded little view of what lay outside. In Pompeii's ruins we may still see one of the first stained-glass window panes—a tiny fragment is set in metal. The catacombs, too, contain a sparse handful of examples, usually in the form of mosaics. Mosaics are thus an ancestor of translucent stained glass.

As time went by, the newly organized Christian Church encouraged experimentation in stained glass, and for hundreds of years the anonymous artisans of the church were the sole practitioners of the craft. They used mosaic technique for the most part, but eventually some craftsman must have decided to try holding his tesserae bits together with strips of lead rather than cement, thus making possible a more transparent effect.

Medieval glass evolved from these beginnings, and even today the products of the twelfth-century glassmakers are considered unmatchable for strange beauty of coloring. Much of this was actually due to the roughness of the glass itself and the primitive manner in which it was created. This crude glass acted as a prism to break up the rays of sunlight in a manner that has never been successfully duplicated, although many craftsmen have tried to wrest the secret from nature. The glass formulas have been forgotten, but the magnificent beauty remains. The glass to be found in the west façade of Chartres Cathedral in France is looked upon by art experts as being the finest ever fashioned by man. In more than eight hundred years it has never been surpassed and quite possibly never equaled.

It is no longer necessary to personally manufacture the basic material; indeed, commercial glassmakers can produce a better and more complete array of hues and colors than can the art-minded craftsman of moderate means. Using this basic material, the artist is then freed to undertake his true challenge—not the making of stained glass, but rather the making of art.

PAINTED STAINED GLASS

Versatile Dek-All is often used to simulate stained glass colors. This medium is oil-based and can be used as a transparent or translucent color. Glass with a slight textured ripple is best to work upon, since this will help break up the transmitted light by which it is viewed. The Dek-All is mixed with its special Trans-Mix and a little thinner, then applied directly to the glass surface. You can design freehand or work over a water-colored guide placed beneath the pane. The colors will become very durable. Once dry, insert the panes into your window with standard putty, decorated sides inward, or, for temporary use, tape them over the existing clear panes. With little expense you have created a distinctive window for your home, church, or store display window.

This method is a simple, popular approach to stained glasscraft. A more advanced project is now offered for readers who wish to create permanent renditions, following the general procedure of traditional stained-glass making.

TRADITIONAL STAINED GLASS

Depending on your personal taste, you may make stained glass windows, wall hangings, skylights, or tabletops from simple rectangles of window glass, or try the more complicated version which resembles a mosaic of broken fragments. Obviously, working with the simple panes "as is" will prove far easier than joining odd-sized pieces. The latter method, however, is closer to historic cathedral glass.

The first step is to select glass of uniform thickness and thoroughly clean it. Unless you are creating an abstract pattern, it will now be necessary to make a design.

Working actual size, sketch up a number of motifs and consider how well they will integrate with the available space and lighting source. Plan for proper facing of the principal subjects; forms should face toward the center of interest. If there are to be three windows, for example, the center one should normally face toward the observer, and those on either side toward the center.

The sketch (i.e., cartoon) is drawn on white paper, then colored in, using any handy medium. This will serve as your guide.

The next step is to divide the motif into segments. Draw in heavy black lines with India ink or charcoal to simulate the traditional leading that holds the design bits together. Handling molten metal is unnecessary, so we will substitute the use of grouting for the lead or solder of the historic technique when, later, we assemble the stained glass.

Your motif should always be a relatively simple one, avoiding complicated intermixing of colors, for remember: your coloring will consist of cut pieces of glass, not freehand art. The theme is a matter of personal choice. Some possibilities: religious subjects and symbols; geometric shapes; animal and bird forms; stars, sun, and moon; landscapes, leaves, and nature forms; snowflakes; flowers; portraits; skyscrapers.

Plan the placement of the leading lines to avoid cutting into the middle of some basic shape. Restrict your colors so that only one is applied within any fragment of glass.

Now lay the color guide face up on a table and place a sheet of plain glass on top. Using a grease pencil, trace an outline of each design segment and then identify it by code with the grease pencil. For example, letter a "Y" for yellow, and "R" for red.

You are now ready to cut the glass into the indicated fragments with a glass cutter (available at hardware stores). Wear gardening gloves as a precaution against picking up slivers after cutting. Once the pieces of glass have been cut, refer to the code on them and divide them according to desired color. They are then painted with transparent oil colors on both sides.

After your glass has been stained and dried, reposition the fragments over the cartoon. You will see that they do not quite fit—there is a quarter inch or so of gap between the pieces. These are the areas which were sketched on the cartoon as heavy black lines, the leading or grouting places.

The grouting is now added to hold our jigsaw of bits together. Instead of handling molten lead or solder, we will substitute equally satisfactory

A cartoon is drawn in charcoal or India ink on paper, then colored to serve as a guide for assembling a stained glass window. The sketch is drawn actual size. (*Courtesy Hamilton Wright*)

grouting, made of a choice of available materials. Concrete may be used for large projects, perhaps reinforced with thin strips of steel, cut and laid between to help bind the grouting. You may try ready-mixed *Quik-crete* or a similar mix, which sells for about $1.60 per eighty-pound bag. Just add water, mix to a thick pastelike consistency, and then trowel between the tesserae, smoothing it down with your finger and discarding the surplus. Or, if you prefer to work with bits of colored plastic instead of glass, just cut up sheets of this translucent or transparent synthetic and substitute them for the glass tesserae. Use the commercial adhesive manufactured for Plexiglas as your grout. Fill in the "leading" lines completely, allow the cement to set overnight (or longer, if required); then you may clean away any residue with a scrubbing brush and water. The stained glass section is now ready for framing and mounting.

Child's project in simulated stained glass uses finger-painting technique for temporary decoration. Easter-egg dyes or powder tempera can be mixed with liquid laundry starch and applied directly to window. The paint washes off easily. Black leading is imitated with strips of construction paper pressed on top of the moist paint. (*Courtesy Staley Manufacturing Company*)

Henri Matisse spent the final period of his life designing stained glass windows for a chapel in France. In the picture at left, he sits in front of one of them. At right, painted glass is arranged like tiles in a design by Father Marcolino Maas of Puerto Rico. (*Photos: Wright*)

Scratch-Decorated Glass

Many glass objects found in the home can be scratch-decorated. The procedure: apply oil colors over the glass, let them dry, then scrape out designs with a sharp instrument, re-exposing the clear glass beneath. You can then add a contrasting color on the back of the glass, so that it will show through the scratched areas. The opaque or translucent oil colors will effectively hide any irregularities, so it is not important to labor over the hidden side. We suggest gold or silver interior painting to show through a darker color on the outside.

The tools and materials cost little and are quite simple to work with: a sharp-pointed X-acto knife; dark-colored, quick-drying oil or lacquer base paint; a quality one-inch paintbrush (to apply the base color to the glass); white water-color paint or a yellow grease pencil with which to sketch the initial design on the glass; and gold-colored Tip On, a lacquer touch-up paint obtainable at paint or hardware stores. Your glass object can be a glass-covered picture frame, glass ash tray or candy dish, wide-necked vase or any decoratively shaped bottle whose neck is wide enough to permit your brush to be inserted and controlled.

Through our scratch-decorating technique, ordinary picture frames can be transformed into unique serving trays, the lowly ash tray or glass candy dish becomes a splendid, personalized gift, and a wide-necked vase or

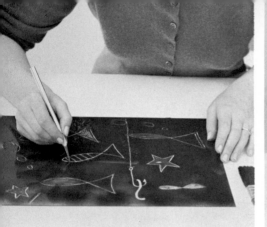

Scratch-decorated glass. Motif is scratched with a sharp knife through a dry ground coat of dark paint. Exposed lines are then covered with gold lacquer. When glass is turned over, design shows through as gold tracery against dark background. At right, photo shows scratched glass mounted on two trays. Decoration on under side of glass, and glass itself, is protected by a plywood base.

bottle becomes an attractive accessory for the home. The steps for transforming a picture frame and glass into a handsome party serving tray are as follows:

Remove the cardboard backing of the frame and expose the glass. Clean the glass carefully with soap and water. Using dark, quick-drying oil or lacquer base paint, paint one side of the glass, stroking carefully with a quality brush. Lacquer spray paint may also be used, and it dries rapidly.

When paint is fully dry, sketch on the design with white water-color paint and a camel's-hair brush (or you may prefer a yellow grease pencil). Sketch the motif on the surface of the black-painted background. With a sharp-pointed X-acto knife, next scratch the design by cutting directly into the black paint, exposing the glass under-surface. Fine scratch lines combined with heavier, bolder lines add unusual interest to the over-all design.

When completed, wipe away all traces of the water-color paint or grease pencil with a soft cloth. Only the dark covering base paint remains, contrasting with the exposed glass areas of the design.

Working on the same side of the glass, next cover the exposed glass portions of the design with gold-colored Tip On.

When fully dry, simply reverse the glass, placing the painted side against the backing, and remount in the frame. Cover the underside of the tray with a section of soft felt to prevent its scratching furniture when the tray is used. Decorative serving handles may be added or the tray used as is. The glass surface can be washed without harming the durable design.

An inexpensive ashtray is turned into a conversation piece by scratch-decorating. Bottom is protected by a glued-on square of thin felt.

This same technique can be used to decorate ash trays and glass candy dishes; always apply the design to the underside. With wide-necked vases and bottles, the design is applied to the inside by working through the neck of the vase or bottle.

Etching on Glass

Engraving on glass is a skilled procedure and its practice by professional means is usually too difficult and costly for the casual hobbyist. Professionals do their etching in one of two ways: by sandblasting through a stencil, or by scratching a design through a wax resist and then applying hydrofluoric acid to the surface of the glass underneath. But sandblasting requires costly equipment, and the acid method is dangerous in inexperienced hands. A much simpler procedure exists, as simple as squirting toothpaste on your toothbrush. The etching agent is a special cream which comes in a tube and costs less than a dollar.

Etching cream makes the decoration of glass so easy and safe that it may be entrusted to children. Most handicraft shops stock it, or it may be ordered by mail from the American Handicrafts, Inc., 12 East 41 St., New York City.

To start, create a design (or trace one onto a sheet of tracing paper). Then place the drawing on top of a sheet of aluminum foil (also available at most hobby stores). Using a hard lead pencil or stylus, retrace the drawing, exerting firm pressure. This transfers the design onto the foil. Then cut out the design from the foil with a razor blade, working on a few layers of thick cardboard to protect your work table.

You now have two stencils—the positive one on the sheet of aluminum foil, and the cutout portion, which can be used for a negative design if desired.

The stencil is next placed on the outer surface of the glassware—which may be a bowl, tumbler, pitcher, bottle, jar, or any other undecorated

STEPS IN ETCHING GLASS THE EASY WAY

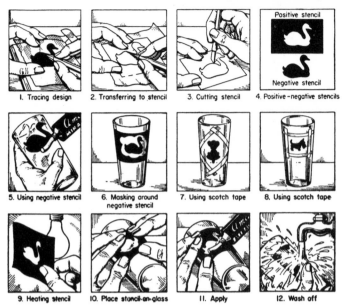

1. Tracing design	2. Transferring to stencil	3. Cutting stencil	4. Positive-negative stencils
5. Using negative stencil	6. Masking around negative stencil	7. Using scotch tape	8. Using scotch tape
9. Heating stencil	10. Place stencil-on-glass	11. Apply	12. Wash off

object. Keep the design from slipping by pressing down on the foil with the bowl of a spoon (i.e., burnishing technique) or by rolling a round lead pencil firmly across the foil. Another way is by warming the stencil against an electric-light bulb before pressing it against glass. The edges must remain snug against the glass to prevent etching cream from slipping underneath.

The glass surface should be clean and sparkling dry. As soon as the stencil is in place, secure it with masking tape or Scotch tape. Then simply squeeze etching cream from the tube across the exposed areas. After about two minutes, the glass is placed under warm tap water, and the cream washed off. That's the whole story! Your glass is now etched. The stencil can be used again. Take the precaution of wiping it clean and storing it carefully between sheets of flat cardboard.

We have cautioned you to watch that the etching cream does not creep under the edges of the stencil. Generally speaking, this is a good idea, but you may wish to experiment with odd effects and for this purpose you can see what happens when cream does penetrate beneath the mask. The results are unpredictable, but a casual, ragged edge occasionally proves most interesting.

Monograms are etched into glass by use of a special cream (see page 217) applied through a stencil.

Marbleizing on Glass

Marbleizing—a "different" effect for your glassware. Make your own unusual flower vases, ivy bottles, tumblers, and flasks by pouring some Dek-All color straight from the jar into a pan of water. The colors, having an oil base, will float on top of the water in a rainbow hue. By dipping your glass object into the solution (suspended on a string) you will pick up the variegated hues as you lift it free, achieving a marbled effect.

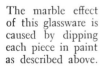

The marble effect of this glassware is caused by dipping each piece in paint as described above.

The proportions of oil color and water are not important, but shake the solution briskly to cause temporary mixing just before you dip. Hang the objects by the string to dry.

Painting on Glass

The most popular method for decorating glass objects is by painting them with oil enamel-type colors. You can do exciting things to cooky jars, drinking tumblers, jugs, and bottles, and if your work is distinctive this type of hobbycraft can become a profitable enterprise. A set of a half-dozen hand-decorated tumblers, for example, might retail for five dollars or more. Regardless of your business acumen, this makes a fascinating avocation and will help brighten your home.

Decorating a set of drinking tumblers is a simple process. The motif is prepared by tracing an original design onto paper, which is rolled, design side out, and then inserted inside the transparent tumbler or wide-mouthed jar. This sketch is repeated directly on the glass surface with your paints. Avoid excessive decoration; restraint is much to be preferred, and the glass itself should dominate. The simple steps are illustrated on page 222.

Since glass that is intended for eating or drinking purposes will be subjected to much handling, it is wise to fire the colors in the kitchen oven at 300° F. for about half an hour to make them more durable.

Working in this same manner, you can create conversation pieces from glass ash trays, cake dishes, condiment containers, salt and pepper shakers, apothecary jars, and any other glass object.

A few pointers on glass decorating. Always clean the object thoroughly before applying color; bits of dirt or the grease from your own perspiration will resist the paint, causing it to flake away at a later time. If a container is painted *inside* and then used for holding food or liquid, heat-treat it to make the colors hard enough to withstand heavy-duty use and dishwashing.

Although glass decorating is disarmingly easy to do, bear in mind that, as with any creative art project, the selection of a proper decorative motif is all-important. Strive for smart simplicity and key the theme to the use of the object. Drinking tumblers will be more appetizing if the colors are tempting, cool in hue, and the artwork appropriate. We emphasize restraint in decorating drinking tumblers because they will contain liquids which have colors of their own. Let the transparency of the glass be a decorative element in its own right. For tumblers, some appropriate themes might be stylized abstractions; fish; sunbursts; ferns; stars and snowflakes; geometric shapes; alphabets; humorous figures; fairy-tale characters; birds and animals; flowers and other graceful, flowing forms.

Hand-painted jars find ready use as cooky jars, flower vases, baby-oil containers, cotton jars, candy holders, bath-salt receptacles, and spice jars. Most department stores now stock inexpensive versions of the old-fash-

Glass jars hand-painted to serve as spice containers. Each carries its own identification in the form of plant from which the spice is obtained.

A cleverly constructed hurricane lamp decorated to match the stencil-screened table linens. Star shapes are painted directly on the glass chimney, which has been placed over an aluminum cylinder that holds candle erect. Holder was soldered onto an old frying pan which has been given a complete coating of white enamel paint. *(Courtesy Prang Studios)*

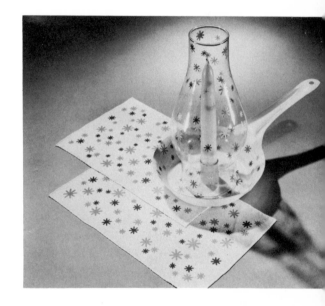

Medicine bottles decorated with Dek-All paint and fired in a kitchen oven at 300 degrees F. for fifteen minutes. Stuck-on wings are Styrofoam. Designed as dressing table companions or to hang on a Christmas tree. *(Created by Art Tanchon)*

[221]

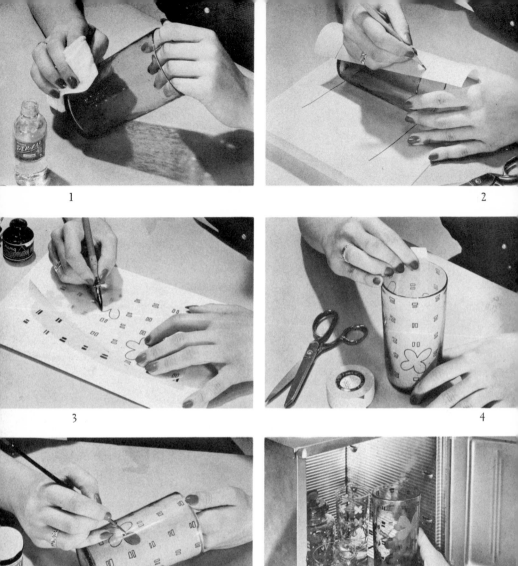

Steps in decorating a glass tumbler. 1. Clean surface thoroughly with soap and warm water. Polish dry, making certain no fingerprints remain. 2. Roll tumbler with sheet of white paper, mark extremities, then flatten paper and rule out area which rolled-up paper would occupy inside glass. Sketch design on it. 3. Place transparent acetate film over design, and outline with India ink. 4. Cut and slip acetate sheet inside glass, and tape to hold. White paper inserted behind acetate will show pattern better. 5. Paint with oil-base colors (such as Dek-All) is applied directly to outside of glass. 6. Finally place glass in kiln (or kitchen oven) at moderate heat to harden oil colors. (*Courtesy Prang Studio*)

ioned apothecary and candy jars. These should be entirely free of any decorative art, of course. Exclusive gift shops sell hand-decorated jars of this type for ten times the cost of the blank glass variety. So why not do your own decorating?

Hand-Decorated Christmas Ornaments

This Christmas, when you make out your gift list, plan to give of *yourself*, by creating things of lasting beauty. Glassware in particular has function as well as decorative charm. A set of hand-decorated tumblers can be personalized by painting on a theme in the holiday spirit and adding the recipient's name in a handsome script. Or decorate pitchers, cake plates, sets of salt and pepper shakers, and mug and saucer sets for the small fry. Design a boxful of glass ornaments, each one decorated with a

Votive lamps for a chapel painted in Dek-All by Madeline Hasse of Los Angeles' Immaculate Heart College. *(Photo: Christy-Shepherd)*

Christmas balls in solid colors gain character when painted in home-made designs. Dek-All paint adheres to surface. Stick necks into modeling clay to hold while decorating.

choice of motifs that includes stylized holly, evergreen branches, a house and steeple, snowflakes or stars. Other ornaments can be cut from sheets of soft, transparent Lucite with a sharp knife. These plastic shapes are hand-decorated as abstract holiday symbols or as naturalistic animal and plant forms. A small hole drilled in their tops will serve as a point for fastening them to the tree with a length of colored ribbon or a metallic string.

Glass balls, either transparent or solid-colored, should be purchased undecorated. They are fragile, so clean them gingerly with a soft cloth, then apply the design through a stencil or work freehand. Hold the ball in your hand and apply oil-base colors with a camel's-hair water-color brush. (You can stick the ornament's base in a block of modeling clay to hold it firmly and free both hands.) Use a separate brush for each color. The ornaments should not be fired; they will normally be handled with care and are not subject to much wear.

You may also dip the balls into a solution of Dek-All floated on top of a pan of water. This will create a multi-colored, marbleized effect. Or lightly coat them with thin glue and sprinkle on glitter.

A final suggestion for decorating glass balls: dip a toothbrush into your color and, using a knife or your finger, spatter the color onto the ball. (Keep the toothbrush about six inches away and the tiny dots of color will be uniform in size.)

City of Glass

An inexpensive glass dish is transformed into an exciting wall panel in a matter of minutes! The same procedure is used to make glass inserts for decorating cigarette boxes and jewelry chests. The cloisonnée effect is achieved by applying oil color across the entire glass surface with a damp sponge. Additional textural effects are created by pressing string against the wet, thick color, or by tooling with a pencil.

When the undercoating is dry—about fifteen minutes—the city buildings are added on top by painting with Dek-All, used opaque (i.e., unmixed, directly from the jar). Build up the cityscape for a three-dimensional effect and add shadows with dark, opaque lines. Details are finally rendered with thin black lines.

The glass plate can be mounted on your wall with a dish bracket or leaned against the backrest of a hutch or cupboard. If the dish is flat-bottomed, it can be cemented onto a block of polished wood and used on tables as a paperweight or container for paper cups, pencils, et cetera. Allow an inch of wood to show around it as a frame. For extra durability, fire the unmounted glass plate in your kitchen oven at 300° F. for fifteen minutes.

The project is also applicable to prefired tiles which may be used as a border or facing on a fireplace and as simple decorative pieces.

City of glass. An ordinary glass dish or ash tray can become a distinctive kind of wall panel to be hung "as is" or mounted on a thin block of wood for framing. Cloisonnée effect is achieved by applying oil-base paint to entire surface as a background, patting it on with a sponge for rough texture. Undercoating is allowed to dry; then design is painted on with contrasting opaque oil colors. (*Courtesy Prang Studios*)

23

Popular Art Techniques

Water Color

ALTHOUGH USUALLY a favorite technique of the amateur artist, water color is one of the more difficult art mediums to handle properly. It demands sureness of touch, complete control, and careful planning before the first stroke is applied to the paper surface. Unlike oil paints, water color cannot be easily corrected. Color must be removed before it sinks into the paper fibers, and such removal is more a matter of dilution with water than erasure. Do not use white to cover mistakes, as it robs the work of its clear brilliance and transparency. For this reason, a water color should be deliberately planned.

This does not mean that the work is to be painstakingly applied. On the contrary; a good water color, by the very nature of its nonerasability, should be painted very quickly and with bold, freehand strokes of the brush.

Beginners are encouraged to select large brushes and to paint in as carefree a manner as possible. Control comes later, but the primary consideration must be to flow on color generously.

Again, unlike oil painting, which allows the artist to experiment directly on the canvas by intermixing and scrubbing on his paints, the water-colorist must do his mixing *before* applying his tints. While water colors can

[226]

be overpainted, one over another, the results are less mixtures than the showing through of the various layers. Thus the colors should be blended on your glass or porcelain palette first, then diluted as necessary with clean water, until the required hue is attained.

Always select brushes of good quality. Children may find a ten-cent brush acceptable, but the serious beginner can make no more sensible investment than a set of well-shaped, carefully constructed brushes. There is little point in putting hours of work into an effort and then finding that the strokes are ragged, the brush hairs are caught in the dried color, and control is completely lost because of an investment in false economy. No artist is any better than his tools allow.

Make it a habit to wash out your brushes after each painting session. Dried color will shorten the life of your brush. Always wash with plain

"Locomotive." Water color by Dong Kingman. (*Courtesy Midtown Galleries*)

These water-color brushes meet most requirements. From left to right: no. 12 (for large details); no. 8 (for average details requiring broad strokes); no. 4 (for general work); flat brush for sweeps of color; stiff bristle brush, which is similar to those used in oil painting and can apply stippling strokes. (*Courtesy M. Grumbacher, Inc.*)

tap water, gently squeeze out excess water, shape the brush, and hang it hair-down on a holder, or store it flat. If the brushes are to be put away for a length of time, you should add a few camphor flakes to the container. More detailed information about brushes and their care is given in Chapter 25 under "Brushes."

Water colors are chiefly a transparent medium, although there are some opaques available. Opaque water colors, however, are mostly used by illustrators and other commercial artists who block in large areas and desire a smooth, more or less solid appearance.

Water colors come in three forms: cakes, tubes, and powdered color. Any form is satisfactory, regardless of your status as an artist. Cakes are economical and easiest to handle and store. Tubed colors are sometimes of higher quality, but they will eventually dry out. They can be intermixed by squeezing them onto a glass mixing palette like oil paints and diluting with water before applying to the paper. Powdered color must be stored in an airtight container or it will pick up moisture and turn into a crude cake. These colors are the least costly.

Equipment for the water-colorist should include these basic tubed colors or their caked equivalents: alizarin crimson, cadmium yellow light, yellow ochre, cadmium red light, Thalo or Hooker's green, light red, ultramarine, cobalt blue, burnt sienna, burnt umber, and ivory black.

If you choose a box of caked colors, it usually contains its own mixing palette. If you prefer tubed colors, you'll need a paintbox with compartments and a lid which acts as the mixing palette. In all cases, have a good-sized jar with a screw top to hold water, a sponge for wetting the paper, and a decent assortment of brushes. Some painters use a small dish and draw water from the large jar to avoid contaminating the main supply.

A form of water color with great versatility is casein paint. Depending on how it is applied, casein can simulate a delicate water-color wash, thick tempera, or oil paint. It is, however, a water-base color, which dries quickly and forms a permanent, waterproof finish.

Your paper can be chosen from many available sizes, types, and weights, as individual sheets, or in book or block form. The lighter weights are the least expensive in most cases. Papers will range from 72-pound up to as high as 300-pound weight. A good average weight of 140 pounds is suggested for fairly large paintings; its greater weight prevents sagging, wrinkling, and buckling. There is cold pressed paper (smooth) and hot pressed paper (rougher). Most water colorists seem to favor the moderately rough varieties. It can take more abuse and some degree of inadvertent scrubbing as well as impart a textural effect.

The sheets of water-color paper should be either tacked tightly onto a solid wood drawing board or stretched across the wood frame if you are easel-painting. The frame is a wood rectangle—actually a plain, flat picture frame—and you stretch your paper across it, tacking the excess paper in the back.

Young artists can do their early water colors on inexpensive newsprint or wrapping paper. In fact, the use of printed newspapers as a painting surface can produce unusual textural effects, much like a collage. Professionals have often done just this. Newspapers also make a fair palette on which youngsters can mix their tones. Other acceptable palettes are a plain white dish, a sheet of window glass, or a sheet of aluminum foil.

Experimenting in water color is always an interesting adventure. For example, a few basic tricks of the trade of value to the neophyte:

To achieve a hard edge to your strokes, paint directly on dry paper. To create a free-flowing effect, dampen the paper's surface with a water-impregnated sponge and then brush on your colors so that they virtually float across the surface before sinking into the paper.

Avoid using erasers on a water color; they are too hard on the delicate paper and once a tint has been lightened, it is difficult to match.

For gradations of color tone, load the brush with water, then put a dab of pure color on the tip and stroke the color on, using the side of the hairs. For continuous washes of the same tone, use a broad brush, and work back and forth lightly at a uniform speed.

Textural effects can be added to a water color in a large variety of ways. White highlights can be lightly scratched with a razor blade. (Do this only when you are certain of the results, for once the paper is scraped, you cannot apply additional color on top of these areas or the pigments will dry in the depressions, leaving ragged marks.) You can pat a sponge across the painting, loaded either with color or just with water, to add a textural effect. Or you can paint one tone on top of another quickly, to create a spreading blend. This, however, will prove accidental; only much practice and experimentation can assure you of any degree of selectivity in such a procedure.

Among your early experiments you will want to explore the use of water color mixed with opaque white. The resulting tones will be semiopaque. Use white sparingly and never to create pure whiteness. White on a water color is usually just a matter of *not* applying color to the paper. And remember—there are few rules in any form of painting which cannot be deliberately ignored for the sake of experimentation. You can paint with a brush, a sponge, your fingers, sticks, or even color-dipped pieces of string.

Tempera

Tempera color is also known as poster paint or show-card color. It is quick-drying, inexpensive, and opaque. It comes in concentrated liquid-like form (to which you may add water for dilution), or as powder tempera. Powdered color is quite popular for school use, being the least expensive and the best for prolonged storage. It is easily removed from hands and clothing with soap and water. Mistakes are corrected by waiting until the color dries, then painting on top of the errors. Since tempera is opaque, all colors beneath are obviously hidden. White tempera is the usual color control, especially for evening up irregularities in lettering against a white poster stock, which is the most common.

Recommended basic palette of colors for average use: red, yellow, green, blue, black, and white. Other available hues include purple, brown, orange. The colors can be intermixed in jars or pans to create almost any other hue. Store liquid tempera in tightly screwed jars, and avoid getting the lip of the jar wet with color, as this will make it difficult to reopen. Paint-sealed containers may be loosened by scraping with a knife or tapping along the edges.

Tempera can be combined with a water color to establish solid areas and for special effects. The colors are relatively permanent, but are subject to cracking. Where water color sinks into the paper, tempera adheres to the surface. Tempera also has a tendency to rub off with excessive handling. This can be prevented by adding some library paste to the color when mixing. Use tempera colors for making posters, for opaque effects in mixed media paintings, to decorate cardboard boxes and wooden toys, and as a handy form of finger paint.

"Sun Tan." Egg-tempera painting by Zoltan
Sepeshy. (*Courtesy Cranbrook Academy of Art*)

Oils

Oil painting is the universally popular technique which is regarded as
the ultimate in artistic endeavor. Because the majority of master paintings
have been done in this medium, it is erroneously considered suitable only
for skilled individuals. This is not necessarily so. True, it is a medium
demanding great control. It is also one of the more expensive with which
to work—top-quality oil colors may cost upwards of several dollars per
tube. And it is not recommended for young people who might put its
sometimes-toxic pigments in their mouths. (It cannot be removed from
clothing easily.) However, no imaginative artist will feel content until he
has tried to master the technique. It is permanent art. A properly executed oil painting can endure for centuries.

Oil paints are really among the easiest to handle. Mistakes can be corrected. If you are really impatient, you can load fresh color onto the
canvas, completely covering your errors. Or you can scrape away the paint
with the palette knife or a cloth moistened with turpentine. Avoid excessive correction in this manner. Instead, plan before you paint. When the
oil color has dried, you may overpaint, but remember—it takes quite a
while and you want always to bear in mind that it is better to remove
color than to work on a soft coating. But don't fall into the habit of excus-

ing bad technique and lack of control for the sake of "experimentation." Learn to master the art form, not to bend it to suit your purpose.

Canvas for painting is sold by the square yard, ready to be stretched over a frame and tacked taut. Stores also sell canvas already stretched in a number of standard sizes. Raw canvas must first be sized, then given a ground coat of white lead and a little linseed oil or a similarly toned paint. This keeps the oil colors from sinking into the raw canvas and gives you a plain background on which to sketch your art. (Follow the same procedure if using wallboard.) The ground coat should be allowed to dry for a decent interval before beginning your painting. Therefore, the wise artist prepares a number of canvases well in advance and stores them, properly wrapped to remain clean. Canvas must be stored in a reasonably warm room; excessive cold will cause the surface to crack, particularly if the canvas is in a roll.

An old canvas which has previously been painted can be reused by following this procedure: (1) Scrape down the ridges of paint with a razor or palette knife until the surface is smooth. (2) Sandpaper surface. (3) Apply a new ground coat of white lead paint, slightly cut with copal oil varnish to speed drying time. This can be applied with a large brush or, better, with a palette knife. Allow it to dry completely before starting the new painting.

Or you may prefer to paint on Masonite, a hard board. Either side of the board is acceptable. The smooth side is good for free-flowing application with your brushes; the canvaslike back side is just as satisfactory, although it does require a heavy ground coat.

While some artists can paint directly on the canvas with no preliminary ado, most professionals prefer to make careful sketches before they start the picture. These are then followed to make an initial sketch on the working surface. You may sketch your art with a charcoal stick or pencil or use greatly thinned paint and draw the sketch with a brush.

Oil colors are mixed on a palette, usually made of wood or glass. (Any plank of wood is suitable after it has been sanded smooth and given a sealing coat of shellac.) Or use a sheet of window glass, placed on your worktable, with a sheet of white paper beneath to offer contrast, so that you can readily see your pigments. The oil colors are squeezed generously onto the palette, allowing a couple of inches between the puddles of paint. This is the working supply, which can be mixed (using a palette knife) with other colors, diluted with turpentine, or made more slow-drying by adding linseed oil.

As with water color, select brushes of good quality. Oil brushes must be stiffer than water-color brushes because oil paints are thick substances. Select varying sizes, ranging from a fine style through medium widths and including at least one brush of one-inch or larger hair span. The basic oil-color brushes are:

Round Bristle. For textural effects where a rough or stippled surface is desired. Is properly held close to the ferrule, the handle against the palm, your grip closed about it as though shaking hands.

Round Sable. Best used to depict fine lines. Hold loosely near far end of handle to create free flowing lines. For minutely precise detail work, hold it like a pencil, close to ferrule.

Flat Sable. Good choice for glazing a painting and for imparting a high finish. Works best on smooth surface like gesso panel. Also good for superimposing one color over another without disturbing the passage just painted.

Filbert. Combines a number of the features of the round and flat bristle brushes. A soft sable filbert is resilient and thus can be used when doing a casein underpainting for which water is used as the medium. It does not tend to pile up paint like many other brushes, and is therefore recommended when an underpainting must be kept thin. Adapts itself to all painting mediums.

Long-Hair Bristle. One of two "workhorses" for painters; with the short-haired bristle it does much of any oil painting. Its flexibility produces a fluid brush stroke.

Short-Haired Bristle. Has tendency to dig into a previously painted wet surface. Best used for direct painting outdoors when speed is necessary. The edge can make a fine line.

Outline Brush. A flat bristle brush, useful for drawing in the composition on your canvas prior to painting. Also used to outline areas. Edge can be used for fine to medium lines, depending on heaviness of stroke.

Back-of-Brush. Here's where your old, worn-out brushes can be put to use. The rear tip is a textural device on wet paint and may be used similarly to the knife. Its coarse line is often used to depict grass and foliage. Most effective on a heavily painted surface.

Except as indicated above, hold a brush several inches back from the ferrule, not like a writing pen or pencil. Grasp the brush handle as though lightly shaking hands with it. Always work in a dust-free area, with plenty of light. Do not crowd close to the area. Move back from the easel or drawing board at intervals as your work progresses so that you can inspect all portions of the painting as an integrated unit rather than as spotty details seen close up.

Oil brushes should be cleaned promptly when work stops; do not allow paint to remain on them for any length of time, or the color will cake rock-hard. Although caked oil color may be removed with acetone (an alcohol derivative), the brush can seldom be used again for any delicate work. Play it safe and rinse the brush in turpentine, then wash it thoroughly in warm water with soap, dry gently on a clean cloth, and store as you would a water-color brush. With good oil brushes ranging in price from a dollar to perhaps ten dollars or more, it is foolish to endanger your investment because of laziness. Clean promptly. Also, whenever possible, reserve a different brush for each different color during painting. This will save time and the wear of repeated rinsing and rubbing clean.

The palette of colors is entirely up to the artist. A representative selection would range through the spectrum—violet, blue, green, yellow, orange, red, plus white, black, and some earth colors (that is, reddish-browns, which are particularly useful for flesh and nature tones). It is not the purpose of this book to delve into the finer details of oil painting; obviously, your personal selection of colors can include many subtle variations of these basic colors, and part of the pleasure of oil painting lies in browsing through an art supplier's stock, reveling in the enticing array of hues which are available.

"Flowers and Stormy Sky." Oil painting by Henry Schnakenberg. (*Courtesy Kraushaar Galleries*)

"Divertissement." By Eugene Berman. (*Courtesy Julien Levy*)

The most popular form of oil color comes in tubes. These are available as student or professional colors, with the higher-quality types naturally being finer, more costly, and more adaptable. The most widely used size is the studio tube, which measures about four inches in height by an inch in diameter. Except when used *alla prima* (straight from the tube), oil colors are usually intermixed to create the desired tints, and this mixture is extended with zinc white. Smaller tubes are manufactured for personal hobbycraft use. Oil colors take a long time to dry thoroughly. Actually, even when a painting seems to be dried, bear in mind that this is only the surface and that an oil painting dries inward and may take months or even a year to dry fully. Therefore, an oil painting should not be given its final varnish or shellacking for at least six months. Oil paintings may be rendered with the brush, palette knife, or fingers. Surface texturing is done by building up the paint layers and by scratching.

[235]

Unused oil paint can be salvaged from your palette by scraping it off with a palette knife, placing the color under water in a dish or pan until it is needed again.

Oil paints are removed from the hands with turpentine followed by a good scrubbing with soap and warm water. You can also buy a special cream which is rubbed over your hands before you paint and thus makes stain removal easy.

A tube of oil color can be used to the last available drop by adapting the practice of squeezing the tube from the base upward and rolling it as you progress.

Sometimes your tube of oil color will have too much oil floating along the top. If you wish to remove this excess, put the squeezed color on absorbent paper (paper toweling or newspaper) for a few moments, then transfer it to the palette.

Additional equipment for oil painting would include an easel, of wood or aluminum. Heavy and strong wood easels are preferred for studio work, aluminum and lightweight for painting on location. You should also, of course, have turpentine on hand for diluting colors. A flexible palette knife is useful for mixing colors and sometimes for applying the color directly to the canvas if you wish to experiment with this technique.

Chalk and Pastel

These are soft materials and must be sprayed with fixative for permanency. Pastels are quality chalks to which binder has been added. In this form they are worthy of serious artistic application in their own right and can be among the more durable drawing materials. Delicacy of hue and subtle blendings (made with the fingertip or a paper and cotton stump) are characteristic advantages of pastel for sketching studies and portraiture. Special papers with a velvet finish are manufactured for pastel work, but any rough-surfaced stock is acceptable.

Low-cost chalks are universal favorites. Some, more expensive, are manufactured in fluorescent colors that glow provocatively under light (daylight or, in special brands, under black light, for more spectacular applications). But the garden variety will keep youngsters happy for hours on end. You can create your own chalkboard out of heavy cardboard with an overcoating of flat black paint. A damp rag will wipe the surface relatively clean. Chalks may also be rubbed through cutout stencils, providing a decorative material which may be transferred onto paper and wood.

Want to make your own chalk? Take powder tempera and mix it with a little water and plaster of Paris or molding plaster. Then press a stick or pencil into a block of modeling clay, creating molds into which the pasty liquid can be poured until it hardens.

Pastel portrait by Robert Brackman shows softness and delicacy possible in this chalklike medium.

Charcoal

Charcoal comes in the form of crude sticks, chunks, and as the filling in pencils. It is excellent for rapid sketching on rough papers or as guidelines for oil painting, and can be rubbed across a sheet of tracing paper to transfer art work onto other surfaces. Just retrace the lines onto the object, using a stylus or hard pencil. Thick sticks of charcoal are widely used in art classes for sketching, using large sheets of dull paper. A piece of chamois skin is a handy accessory with which to blend, modify, and erase charcoal lines. Kneaded erasers are also used, primarily to pick out highlights. Charcoal can be fixed with the same fixative used for chalk and pastels. It is blown onto the work through an inexpensive atomizer—either by hand pressure through a bulb, or by mouth through a pipette. You can make your own fixative by mixing white shellac and alcohol. When blowing on the fixative, work in a well-aired room and keep the sprayer about a foot or so away from the working surface. Avoid heavy concentrations of fixative; it is preferable to blow it on lightly and, if required, repeat the spraying a few times. The charcoal will darken slightly, then dry durably in a few minutes.

Caricature of Daniel R. Fitzpatrick made in grease pencil on rough textured paper by David Low.

Projects with Pencils

Certainly no tool for graphic expression is more universally used than the pencil. Pencils come in a large variety of shapes and styles, ranging from soft graphite to hard tracing kinds.

For art use, the most popular pencils are flat carpenter's graphite sticks, used for shading large areas of sketches and layouts; Wolff pencils, for adding crisp details to renderings and portraits (often combined with chalks and pastels which create the tones over which the accents are thus added); charcoal pencils, for preliminary sketching of large renderings which may then be completed in oils or similar opaque mediums; and colored pencils which are portable and mess-free in the youngest artist's hands. A pack of colored pencils and a sketch pad are all the equipment you really need for on-the-spot sketching where color notes are important.

Colored pencils of good quality are usually water soluble, which means that any art can later be brushed with water and turned into an aquatint.

Commercial artists find that a soft graphite pencil can be used over various types of paper, mat board, cardboard, and even the back of a sheet of Masonite to produce distinctive textured effects not possible with any other medium. The softness of the graphite picks up every depression and raised area inherent in the material beneath, creating excellent built-in highlights and shadows, stippled or tweedy textures for clothing and background patterns. Try drawing your fashion art on white bond paper with pen and ink, then slip a sheet of corrugated cardboard, Masonite, or sandpaper underneath and add textural effects by rubbing a soft pencil or stick of charcoal in the desired areas. With a bit of experimentation

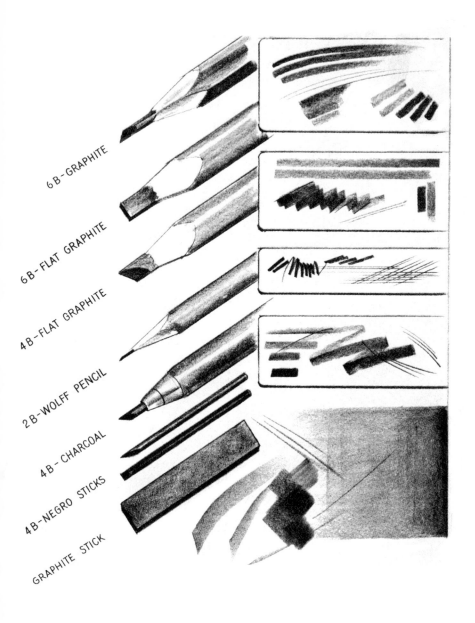

6B-GRAPHITE

6B-FLAT GRAPHITE

4B-FLAT GRAPHITE

2B-WOLFF PENCIL

4B-CHARCOAL

4B-NEGRO STICKS

GRAPHITE STICK

Different pencils, charcoal and graphite sticks are shown with demonstration strokes next to them. *(From Rendering Techniques for Commercial Art and Advertising by Charles Kingham, Courtesy Reinhold Publishing Corporation.)*

you can produce the appearance of a mink stole, tweed cloth, Scotch plaid, glazed satin, and many similar materials.

Most art-agency roughs and visualizations are done with either brush and ink or pencil and gray tones of Nu-Pastel. All pastel, charcoal, and pencil renderings should always be sprayed with fixative to prevent smudging.

BLOCK PRINTING AND THE PENCIL

Sketches for linoleum and wood-block carving are customarily drawn on thin tracing paper with a soft graphite pencil; then the tracing sheet is turned over, positioned on the block, and traced through with a sharp hard pencil. The soft graphite is transferred by this pressure onto the light surface of the block in crisp, neat lines which can then be carved out as desired.

PENCIL STENCILING

Lightly stroke colored pencils within the cutout areas of your stencil, working for broad masses by holding the tool at an angle and using its side. (You may sandpaper the long "lead" flat to facilitate this application.) If you wish to impart a textured effect, place rough fabric beneath the drawing paper, or use corrugated cardboard, or the rough side of a sheet of Masonite. Then, to impart a smooth effect, rub the colored areas with a piece of cotton or a tortillon stump. (This stump is made of compressed and rounded paper or felt.) Delicate gradations of light and dark values are made possible by changing the amount of pressure used.

FINGER BRUSHING

Chamois, felt, or flannel may be cut and sewed to form a thimble-shaped tool which is slipped over the index finger for this technique. Then, using soft, colored lead pencils as the medium, rub the thimble across the pencil to pick up color. This is rubbed for tones inside your stencil areas. A larger quantity of powdered pencil color can be made by sharpening the pencil and dumping the powder into a dish.

POWDER-PUFF STENCILING

Using colored pencil dust, press a powder puff into the medium and pat inside the stencil openings. If you wish a textured effect, cover the powder puff with a paper napkin or piece of rough fabric and apply.

24

New Uses for Scrap Materials

Don't throw away that leftover bottle, piece of tinsel from last year's tree, or pocketful of acorns Junior hid in his desk. It can be put to imaginative use!

There are a thousand bits of bric-a-brac around any home and classroom which could head for the ashcan under what we call normal circumstances. Before you start throwing things away, though, read this chapter. Could be you're thinking of tossing away hidden treasure. Here are some things to do with them.

Acorns, Seeds, and Nuts

Ever think of making necklaces and bracelets by boring a hole through them and inserting a colored string? Little children would delight in a miniature doll's set of cup and saucers made by scooping out the acorn meat and using the shell for the saucer. The acorn itself is sawed off about a third of the way down, scooped out, and used to hold "tea" for a little doll. You can also make dolls entirely of strung nuts and acorns. (Try using pipe cleaners to join the movable parts.) Cooked horse chestnuts make a simple kind of library paste. Another necklace idea: combine acorns and hollow chunks of uncooked macaroni, alternated along a string. Fill a fabric bag with acorns or seeds to make a toss bag. Glue seeds, shells, and acorns to a hand-decorated piece of cardboard to make unusual greeting cards.

Shells

Clamshells and other sea shells make excellent ashtrays, buckles, beads, buttons, darning eggs, inlays on cigarette or jewelry boxes! They are cleaned and brightened by dipping them into a weak solution of hydrochloric acid (wear rubber gloves and keep the solution very dilute). Polish them with putty powder to a high luster. Ceramists can grind up sea shells into a fine powder which can be mixed with unfired clay to hasten the firing.

Tinsel and Aluminum Foil

Foil that has been reclaimed from broken ornaments by hammering with a wood mallet can be reshaped to new decorations for your holiday tree. And you can paint them if you like. Rolls of foil from the neighborhood grocery can be stamped out in designs with cooky cutters. These, in turn, when mounted on cardboard, make fine tree ornaments or mobiles. Mount a sheet on heavy cardboard and then make bas-relief portraits with a dull stylus.

Having trouble with old corks? If the bottle's contents are not alkaline, a twist of aluminum foil will make the cork airtight once more. Use heavy foil to make molds for cement or clay. (The clay can be fired without removing it from the foil. Rub a bit of Vaseline inside the mold first, to prevent sticking, though this seldom happens.) Youngsters can create their own play money by pressing coins into foil and then wrapping the new coin impression around a wooden checker, flat button, or some similar object.

Stains and Dyes

Here's a useful home project, or one for Scouts and art school classes. Boil some alder bark in a copper kettle, then strain the liquid, and you've got a reddish-brown dye for wool or silk. (First boil the fabric in a solution of 1 part alum, 1 part vinegar and 125 parts water, for an hour.) The same dye can be used on raffia, wood, linen, or jute by boiling the desized material for an hour in a solution of 1 part alum, 1 part table salt, and 125 parts water.

Flower or leaf forms are easy to cut from foil or old tin cans for a permanent flower arrangement. *(From How to Make Flower Decorations by Patricia Easterbrook Roberts)*

Daisies made of left over tissue papers rolled and looped into petal outlines. Thin wire holds loops in position and joins flower to heavier wire stems covered with floral tape. Painted buttons form centers. Designed by Patricia Easterbrook Roberts.

Scrap metal or laundry cardboard can be cut into shapes, painted, and assembled to make a mobile. This design is by Fred Dreher.

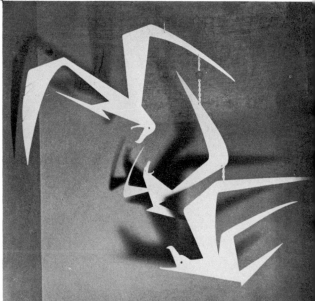

An idea for ends of colored crayons. Make a mosaic picture by cutting crayons to short, even lengths and sticking them down on heavy cardboard. The result can be mounted in an old frame reclaimed from the attic and painted.

Paper plates that are not too soiled can be cleaned and painted for another party or to decorate the playroom mantel. A coat of shellac will give them added durability.

Waterproofing Fabrics

Mix 1 part alum in 40 parts boiling water and add 5 parts sugar of lead to create a cloth waterproofing solution. If you have a plaster cast that is cracking, take this same solution, dilute it further with six parts of water to each one of the solution, and apply to your cast to reharden it.

China Cement

Melt 1 part beeswax with 4 parts rosin powder to make a china cement.

Odd-Sized Blocks of Wood

Got leftovers from a carpentry project? Use them for school carving projects, as lamp bases (decorated with painted designs), shuffleboard blocks (round them on a lathe).

Paper Plates

Paint on clock faces or cut them out into masks. You can decorate paper plates with glue and glitter, glue and shells, poster or oil paint colors, or wax crayons.

Blueprint Paper

You can make prints from negatives on blueprint stock without the necessity of a darkroom. Also good for making silhouettes. Simply expose sheet to sunlight with an object silhouetted in front. Some ideas of subjects for blueprint silhouettes: portraits of students, leaves, flowers, motifs on greeting cards. The paper is then developed in a 10 per cent solution of potassium bichromate.

Old Telephone Books

Put last year's directory to this year's practical use. Tear it to bits and use as basic stock for papier-mâché. Use it to press leaf specimens. Use it as a blotter for mimeographed art work.

Paint-Hard Brushes

Whoa! Is it beyond softening? Then use that handle and the hardened bristles for a sandpaper holder! Just glue on (or use rubber bands) your sandpaper sheet and use the brush as a scraper for reaching nooks and crannies.

Saw off the bristles about an inch from the handle and dip in ink. When scraped with a knife, it makes a spatter printing tool. If the brush is simply old and not hard, use its irregular-length bristles for decorative stippled effects when painting.

Heavy Cardboard Cartons

Got some boxes that originally held TV sets, radios, appliances, mattresses, and such? This tough corrugated stock is splendid for oil painting at low cost and takes oils or caseins as well as wood, Masonite, or other materials do. It is reasonably good for tempera colors. If the stock tends to buckle, it can be reinforced with strips of wood molding.

Use it for constructing model houses, dollhouses, shadow boxes, small exhibits, masks, impromptu frames (when painted and sprinkled with glue and glitter). For classroom fun, cut out areas of the larger cartons to build grocery stores, post offices, and fruit stands. To make more durable and fairly waterproof, apply shellac over art work or decorative motifs.

[245]

Cardboard Tubes

This is the material in which rolled-up calendars come. (Also used in rolls of aluminum foil, toilet paper, and shelving paper.) Use it to make brush handles, to fashion doll or puppet parts. Cut a slot in top edge, plug ends with glued wood pieces or heavy-duty masking tape then paint and shellac it for gay-looking coin bank.

Charcoal

Have you some leftover lumps of charcoal from your fireplace or stubs from sticks that are too small to draw with? Crush them into a powder, add cold cream or cocoa butter, and use for dark makeup. Pour a pile of charcoal powder on a piece of fabric, gather up ends, and tie with string to make a pouncing bag for stenciling. Add shellac to powdered charcoal and you have a permanent marking material for black lines on light surfaces (i.e., sidewalk games, signs in school yard, stencil signs).

Clothespins

Wooden pins make unusual dolls when faces are painted on tops and cloth-scrap clothing is added.

Coffee Grounds

Want stucco effects on miniature buildings or model train tunnels? Just sprinkle grounds over glue.

Celluloid Scraps

Got some bits of broken celluloid from toys, combs, and such things? Dissolve in acetone to make your own model cement.

Pine Cones

Cones may be colored to make unusual tree or package ornaments, lapel pins, heads and bodies for toys, for place-card holders. For extra glamor, brush with glue and sprinkle with metallic or glass glitter.

Opposite: Here four fallen pine cones were combined to make the heads and bodies of two owls nestled in a hollow piece of bark. Dolls, eyes (you could use painted buttons) and sprigs of dried moss and evergreen complete the design by Naida Hayes.

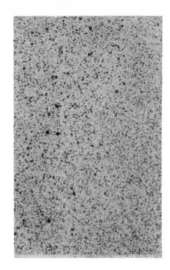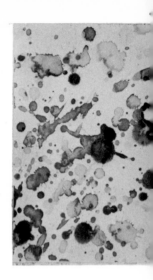

Scraps of white paper can be made into Christmas wrappings, mounts for photographs, or used for permanent box coverings by spattering them with color. Dip a brush in very wet mixture of water color or poster paint, then hit the brush against the forefinger of your other hand so paint spatters over the paper. Repeat with another color when the first spattering is dry. Work area can be protected with newspapers.

Lollipop Sticks

Use as pen holder for quill points by fastening on with strip of masking tape; use to join segments of modeling clay for animal forms; modeling tools when sharpened; masts for toy boats made of soap, with cardboard or painted paper sails; puppet parts.

Milk for Odd Uses

Do you know that condensed milk slightly thickened with flour makes a good temporary paste? Or that skimmed milk, brushed over pencil marks, fixes them permanently? Have you a favorite piece of chinaware that is slightly cracked? Boil it in skimmed milk to nullify appearance of cracks. Skimmed milk also removes ink stains from carpets.

Broken Pen Points

Grind down the end to create an engraving tool for linoleum block cutting or for decorating clay models. Use old ball-point pen as a stylus for embossing on aluminum foil.

[248]

Antiquing Copper with Sal Ammoniac

Sal ammoniac, or ammonium chloride, is available at the druggist. Use a solution of 4 parts sal ammoniac, 3 parts table salt, 125 parts water as a bath for finishing copper artifacts with a fine antique effect.

Sandpaper Paintings

Draw on sheets of sandpaper with wax crayons, then rub a warm flat-iron over this to make an encaustic print.

Felt and ribbon ends can be cut, looped, or otherwise fashioned into charming bouquets to wear or frame as a picture. (*Courtesy Patricia East-erbrook Roberts*)

25

Notes on Materials and Techniques

Alcohol

ALCOHOL IS a solvent which will thin shellac, loosen caked oil paint from brushes, create varnish and cement and that most powerful of solvents, ether. Grease and fat stains on fabrics can be washed off with alcohol. A good cement may be made by dissolving bits of celluloid in alcohol until a thick syrup is attained. By adding more alcohol, this glue thins down to a shellac or varnish which may be brushed and sprayed over artwork and on wood. At the same time, if you wish to loosen glues that have a resinous base, press an alcohol-impregnated rag over the area for a few minutes, then observe the results. In many cases, the cement will have loosened sufficiently to permit separating the bound-together materials. For the most stubbornly caked oil paintbrushes and to dissolve heavy varnishes, the use of ether is recommended as a last resort. Be sure to work in a well-ventilated room and remember—ether is flammable. It is made by the action of sulphuric acid on alcohol. (Do not attempt this chemistry yourself!) Use ether only when nothing else will rescue a valuable brush and even then, exercise precaution.

Artgum Eraser

This soft eraser is used mostly on pencil and charcoal drawings. It crumbles away with the removed pencil lines. Also may be used as a block printer by carving into it with a knife and stamping the carved surface on a rubber stamp, then onto paper or fabric.

Beeswax

A natural product, yellow-brown in color, which, when blended with turpentine, makes an ideal furniture polish. The recipe used by restorers and antique hobby-craftsmen: heat 3 parts of beeswax with 8 parts of spirits of turpentine in a double boiler until the beeswax melts and the turpentine is absorbed into it; then let cool. Apply with soft cloth and rub vigorously until a lovely patina is achieved. Store in airtight tin to keep from drying out.

Bias Binding

A folded strip of cotton material, to be stitched over seams and edges. It makes a good finish for articles made of oilcloth and is obtainable as yard goods.

Brushes

Used for all painting and varnishing projects. Art brushes come in two types:

Water color. A soft-haired brush, usually of red sable, which is numbered according to the hair width. No. 1 is a finely tipped brush for detail work; No. 7 is a medium-sized brush, suitable for working on average sheets of water-color paper or for details on larger paintings; No. 20 is a large brush, suitable for adding broad washes. Brushes used for serious work should be of a good quality. It is false economy to purchase a cheap brush which will break, leave ragged hairs, and otherwise spoil a potentially good painting. A water-color brush is cleaned with water after use and then shaped by running the hairs gently through the fingers. It is hung on a wire rack, tip down, for future use, or, when it will not be used for a while, it should be placed in a box containing some camphor and sealed airtight. Temporary storing with the tips up, in a glass jar, is acceptable, but be certain the individual brushes are spaced so that the air may circulate freely around the hairs and hasten drying. Do not hang brushes upside down while soaking wet; this will cause the moisture to run down into the ferrule, loosening the hairs and eventually causing them to drop out. Never allow the brushes to stand hair-down in a jar. The weight will weaken the natural springiness and misshape the hairs.

Camel's-hair brushes, usually made of cow hair, are very soft. Most low-quality water-color brushes are of cheap camel's-hair type. They are often preferred for children's work because of their modest cost, and may also be used for color notations in the field. Fine-quality camel's-hair brushes are made, but usually it is the sable brush which, because of its spring and durability, is the professional artist's choice. You may also purchase a large camel's-hair brush for dusting.

Oil color. These are stiffer bristle brushes, available in many sizes and styles. Oil brushes should be cleaned promptly in turpentine, then washed thoroughly in warm water and soap, dried gently on a clean cloth, and stored as you would a water-color brush. Caked oil color can be removed with acetone but the brush can seldom be used again for any delicate work. Whenever possible, use a different brush for different colors. See "Oil Painting" in Chapter 23 for more detailed discussion and types of brushes.

Burlap

A coarse, inexpensive material of woven, ropelike threads. Comes in dyed colors or in a natural tan. Useful for making mats, dollhouse rugs, draperies, and as a foundation for hooked rugs. Can also be used for doll clothing and as the body for stuffed toys. Tighter weaves of burlap will hold oil paint and can also be stencil-decorated.

Cambric

A lightweight cotton fabric, suitable for making stuffed toys, bean bags, rag dolls, et cetera. Inexpensive and sold by the yard. Takes crayon and dyes, but not recommended for oil-based colors.

Canvas

A stiff, even-meshed material, suitable for coarse cross-stitching and for running in lines of colored yarn. Most popular use is as painting surface for oil colors.

For the latter use, see "Oil Painting" in Chapter 23.

Carbon Tetrachloride

A noninflammable, colorless solvent, widely used for cleaning fabrics and dissolving grease and oil stains. It has a strong odor similar to chloroform, so use in well-ventilated place. Because of its chlorine content, first test a small area of fabric to determine whether delicate colors might be affected and bleached.

Cardboard

A heavy paper derivative. Bristol board is one popular form, which is used for making charts and maps, posters, and cutout toys. Is stiff enough to act as base for paste-ups and will retain inks and crayon. Oil paints and water colors seldom give a good effect on Bristol because the color sinks in and spreads slightly. For greater strength, use chip board, one of the cheapest forms of cardboard made. (This is the gray cardboard found as backing for note pads.) Chip board makes a good, inexpensive mat and picture mount. May be decorated with poster paints.

Manila tag is another cardboard. It is lightweight, glossy, and ivory in color. It cuts easily with knife or scissors, is popularly used for making booklets, programs, and so forth, but does not have sufficient body to hold shape for heavy construction work. A poor surface for water color. Best decorating mediums on manila tag are crayon and drawing inks.

Fiber board is a heavyweight composition cardboard, used for constructing three-dimensional cutouts, such as nursery wall hangings and jigsaw puzzles. Must be cut with jig saw. Excellent for making low-cost toys, dollhouse walls and roofs. For making windows in dollhouses, first punch a hole in area, then insert saw blade and cut away. Decorate fiber board with oil paints and poster colors. Apply shellac if desired, to protect color.

Chalk

One of the cheapest and most widely known drawing mediums. Comes in many colors, and boxed sets of eight sticks cost only a few cents. May be used on chalkboards or any dull-surfaced paper. Also useful for decorating craft items in wood. Keep a box of colored chalks handy in the glove compartment of your car for on-the-spot sketching with little fuss, while traveling, and to entertain small-fry passengers. Tonal blending is done with fingertips or a soft cloth or paper tissue. Chalk art may be sprayed with fixative to keep from rubbing away. Chalks come in two general varieties, the soft chalk, which is made of alabaster and is the least expensive, and the extruded, dustless type. Dustless chalk is preferred in schoolrooms, for its nonallergic construction prevents particles from floating in the air, it is grit-free, and it helps preserve the chalkboard.

Cheesecloth

A lightweight, loosely woven material which is good for making doll and puppet clothing and school play costumes. Can be use to strain paints which have picked up dirt and lumps.

Clay

Sold in its natural, gray state or manufactured in a large assortment of colors. Natural clay may be dug in many parts of the country, usually being found on stream banks or near iron-ore deposits. Refined clay has been screened of impurities and given a small quantity of oil or Vaseline to help retain its softness. Modeling with clay should thus always be done on newspapers or some protective material to prevent staining the worktable. Other types of clay which are useful to the craftsman are dry clay flour and potter's clay. Directions for obtaining and using clay are given in Chapter 8.

Cotton Batting

A soft material, used to stuff toys, which can be bought at a dry goods store.

Cotton Cord

A hard, lightweight cord, useful for some types of weaving, more commonly used in the form of sewing cotton, for hemming fabrics, sewing seams on rag dolls, and for hanging mobiles.

Crayons

A mixture of wax and coloring pigment, heated together and then pressed into sticks. One of the indispensable art tools for young people. Available almost everywhere in art stores, stationers, drugstores, five-and-dime. Draw on newsprint or any dull-surfaced paper, on plain fabric which has been tightly stretched, on wood objects, and on hardened clay or stone. Can be applied in several different-colored layers, then scratched with sharp tool to reveal successive layers. This is called the sgraffito technique. Melted crayon can be brushed or poured over ceramics as a decorative element. A wax crayon mural can be rendered on muslin, then made permanent and washable by placing artwork wrong-side up on a sheet of smooth wrapping paper and ironing it.

Desizing

The removal of sizing from manufactured cotton fabrics by boiling. This starchy compound, added to give fabric crispness against handling, would resist the application of textile colors if not washed out prior to decorating.

Dyes

Store shelves are well-stocked with trade-named dyes and cold-water tints, all of which are most useful for decorating. Simply dip the fabric to be tinted or dyed into the solution and hang up to dry. Dyes like Tintex are quite safe in the hands of youngsters, and spilled colors will wash out of clothing after several washings. Naturally, do not work with tints or dyes unless wearing old clothes or a protective apron. Cold-water dyes are not permanent. One package will cover many yards of material. The usual procedure: first remove any previous color from fabric with bleach, or use a much darker color over the existing one.

Gesso

A ground for oil paintings, usually applied to canvas or Masonite. Made of gypsum or chalk powder to which glue or casein has been added as a binder, creating a white, thick color. Artists wishing to make their own gesso can use this recipe: one part of gypsum (i.e., lime sulphate) to equal parts of water, glue, and zinc white oil color. Paint this on work surface in thin, even coats, usually about five or six coatings being required to prepare the ground properly. Let each coat dry before the next is brushed on. The drying action is relatively quick. A bit of fine sand may also be added to the mixture to provide *tooth* to the ground. This same gesso mixture can also be brushed onto old furniture and picture frames, over which some gold leaf is applied to create an antique white.

Glue

An adhesive used to bind together materials or wood, cardboard, fiberboard, paper, and so forth. Should be spread over both pieces and then these should be pressed firmly together and weighted until glue sets. A permanent bond may take several hours with the heavier materials. For simple projects use library paste on paper, or, as a somewhat more expensive alternative, use rubber cement. This last-named adhesive is most widely preferred for mounting art on mat backings and making photographic paste-ups. The rubber cement should be spread evenly on the mount and the back of the art, allowed to dry for a few seconds, then the two surfaces pressed together. For a temporary bond—as when affixing the elements of a paste-up for a visual appraisal—just spread rubber cement on the mounting surface and press the dry art in position. Should you then desire to rearrange the art, it will peel up easily. Once the final positioning is achieved, the rubber cement may be spread on the back of the art too, and the permanent bond made. Always store rubber cement in a cool, dry place. When it becomes too thick and picks up a deep orange hue instead of its normal clear color, it may be thinned again with a special thinner sold for the purpose. The thinner is added and stirred until it becomes slightly syrupy in consistency; then the cement is allowed to stand twelve hours before using.

Ink

Ink to the artist means drawing ink, and this in turn usually means India ink. India ink is black, made by adding a gum binder to lamp-black. Drawing inks also come in many colors and may be diluted with water to create washes and tints. Most inks are transparent, but opaque inks are also available. Ink is applied with a pen or brush and it is difficult to erase, although a soft India-rubber eraser can be tried, or even a piece of tightly kneaded fresh bread. Errors can sometimes be lightly scraped away with a sharp razor blade, but be wary of cutting into the paper or new color will fill the scratches and cause them to show up. A little opaque white water color can cover errors too, and if carefully (and sparingly) applied, it is sometimes possible to brush or pen new ink lines over this. Ink drawings should be kept away from heat or strong sunlight, both of which will eventually cause it to fade. Also use ink for string painting, decorating shellacked and lightly sanded wood objects, and for marking leather.

Ivory

A carving or inlaying material usually obtained from the tusks of the elephant or walrus. The carving and color-decorating of ivory is a universal craft. America's New England whalers created beautiful artifacts by carving with fine needles and knives. This traditional folk art is known as scrimshaw and while not generally practiced today, many examples exist in museums and in private collections. It is a relatively costly hobbycraft. The surface of ivory can be polished smooth by using a material called glass-paper, after the surface has been first rubbed with powdered pumice. Ivory is brittle and should not be soaked in water.

Jeweler's Rouge

A high-quality red powder polish used on gold, silver, or other metals. It is chemically obtained by calcining iron sulphate. May be rubbed on dry or mixed with a little water to form a paste.

Leather

Comes from animal skins and is used for binding books, making shoes and belts, and can be hand-decorated with stains or carved. Being organic, it is subject to rotting. To preserve leather, apply a coating of 4 parts alcohol to 6 parts castor oil. Rub in thoroughly and let dry.

Muslin

Unbleached muslin is good for stuffing dolls and making the outer covering. May be glued onto wood or Masonite for mural painting. If block printing on muslin, first remove the sizing by boiling the fabric. Available as yard goods. (See *Crayons* for muslin decorating.)

Oilcloth

A yard-goods material used for inexpensive book covers, the skin of toys and dolls, tablecloths, et cetera. Is waterproof. Edges of oilclothed objects are best protected with bias tape. Can be painted with oil colors.

Oil Color

One of the more permanent of art mediums and historically the most widely used. Comes in literally hundreds of colors and shades. The most popular form of oil color comes in tubes, available as student or professional colors. The most widely used size is the studio tube, about four inches in length by an inch in diameter. Smaller tubes are manufactured for hobbycraft use. Oil colors are usually intermixed to create the desired tints, and this mixture is extended with zinc white. See also "Oil Painting" in Chapter 23.

Papier-Mâché

A term which, translated from its French original, becomes, loosely mashed paper. It is a modeling material, made by boiling paper in water to form a pulp and then adding to this starch or paste and color. Widely used for making window display figures, masks, stage props, puppets and dolls, and similar handcraft items. (See Chapter 1 for full details.)

Pastels

These are the aristocrat of the chalk family. They are excellent for portraiture and sketching and are made permanent by spraying with fixative. They are manufactured like chalk but an oily base of gum tragacanth is added to improve the quality and permanence.

Pencil Crayons

The familiar lead pencil, made in many colors and available in sets or individually. Most better-quality pencil crayons are water soluble, which means the art can be brushed with water to create a water-color effect. (Techniques described under "Projects with Pencils" in Chapter 23.)

Pens

Drawing points are manufactured in dozens of styles and widths for hand lettering, sketching, and precision drafting. The quill pen, as exemplified by the Croquill point, is recommended for delicate linework with India ink; the felt-tip pen (e.g., Flo-Master) is an aluminum-barreled pen with various nibs available to suit the style of freehand drawing or marking desired. Inside the barrel is a quantity of special ink. These fountain-type pens are manufactured in many colors and the nibs are usually interchangeable. The Speedball points are made in many widths and shapes to accommodate practically every drawing or lettering problem.

Plaster of Paris

A plaster compound which is used to make molds of original sculpture, ceramics, or carved materials. The piece is first sized by liberally rubbing petroleum jelly (Vaseline) or liquid soap over its surface to prevent the plaster from sticking when it is applied and later removed. The lubricant is applied with a sponge or the fingers, going over the entire piece two or three times to cover it completely and taking care to eliminate bubbles or pin holes. Then, a retaining wall is built about the piece, allowing ample room between the sides of the wall and the object. A heavy piece of tar paper rolled into a cylinder and held shut with paper clips will do for this, and a flat slab of clay beneath serves as the floor. Apply clay around the joint of the cylinder and the floor to prevent the plaster from seeping out. The plaster may now be mixed with water to a thick, viscous consistency and poured over the object within two minutes, as it dries quickly. Take especial care during pouring to eliminate any air bubbles. (Pouring it over your finger will help.)

When the pouring is completed and the object is completely covered, lift the worktable and tap it down against the floor a few times to further remove any vagrant bubbles. The plaster will set in about ten minutes and must not be touched during this period. It grows increasingly warm during this shrinking (setting) time and after the ten minutes or so, the retaining wall of tar paper may be removed. In approximately a half hour from the time of pouring, the mold may be removed from the original piece by tapping it with a wooden mallet. (Always wrap the piece in burlap to keep from breaking the mold.) Most sculptors drive metal shims into a clay model to help with the separation. The mold should, ideally, be chiseled apart into two sections; but, if it breaks irregularly, the segments can be rescued by soaking them in a pail of water until soft again and then rejoining the pieces with more plaster. Small pinholes still remaining inside the mold are removed with fine sandpaper. Your mold is, thus, a hollow image of the original. When the pieces are locked together with wire or cord, and clay slip (liquid clay) is poured inside (through its open top), you are enabled to cast duplicates. No sizing of the mold is required since the clay will shrink away from the sides during its hardening period.

Pouncing

The procedure of applying color to a drawing surface or object to be decorated by use of a stiff brush or cloth. The color-impregnated tool is pressed lightly and repeatedly over the work surface, holding it perpendicular to the object. Pouncing is often done through a stencil and it may be utilized as a technique to simulate spatter or dry-brush effects.

Punch

A tool available in most stationers and art-supply shops for punching holes in paper, fabric, or leather. The paper circles which are cut out can also be saved to use like confetti for sprinkling over glue-brushed artwork.

Sandpaper

An abrasive used to polish down the surface of wood, ceramics, canvas, and painted materials, preparatory to removal of paint, for finishing or for imparting a patina. When rubbing wood, work only with the grain. Use a sheet of fine sandpaper for sharpening pencil points. Commercial artists usually tack down a few sheets on their drawing board for this purpose. Sandpaper can also be glued or tacked onto a block of wood, which makes a handy holder.

Sand Pictures

A form of graphic portrayal which is generally accredited to the American Indian of the Southwest, but has also been practiced in many other countries throughout history. Basically, various-colored fine sands are dropped by hand onto a glue-covered surface to build up a picture.

Shellac

A resinous substance obtained from the bodies of insects. Commercially manufactured as a mixture of gum arabic and alcohol. When brushed or sprayed onto a surface, the alcohol evaporates, leaving the gum to dry to a hard, permanent, protective coating for paintings, woodwork, and other types of art rendering. It is used to make varnish and should be stored in glass containers rather than tins, to prevent eventual discoloration. Comes in two varieties: clear and orange-colored. Use clear shellac for covering artwork, the orange type for adding a rich and subtle antique effect to woodwork. The latter is also used on wood as a priming coat, preparatory to painting.

Staining

Do not confuse staining wood with shellacking it. Stains seep into the wood deeply, whereas shellac forms a hard surface coating. Stains are used to impart patina and new colors to woods, thus simulating various varieties of wood, such as maple, oak, walnut, or mahogany. The wood grain shows through the stain. To apply, first lightly sand the wood surface until it is smooth and clean, then brush on the stain, or rub it on with a cloth. When stain has dried, rub it lightly with fine sandpaper to bring out the wood grain.

Tempera

The popular coloring medium which usually introduces young artists to the brush-and-paint technique. It is also known as showcard or poster paint and comes as either a powder (to be mixed with water) or in prepared liquidlike form. Tempera colors can be diluted as desired with water to any degree, depending on whether a thick impasto is to be achieved or a thinned down, semitransparent wash. It is the coloring medium which is added to flour or liquid starch to make a low-cost finger paint. Tempera colors are widely used for lettering and artwork on posters. They are easily removed from hands and clothing with soap and water. The colors are reasonably permanent, but have a tendency to flake off cardboard after a while, since they do not sink into the paper surface deeply, but remain on the surface.

Store liquid tempera in tightly screwed jars, and avoid getting the lip of the jar wet with color, as this will make it difficult to reopen. Paint-sealed containers may be loosened by scraping with a knife or tapping along edges.

Textiles

Generally, any woven fabric. Weaving is mostly done with threads of silk, wool, cotton, jute, nylon, or flax. Textiles are cleaned by preliminary use of a vacuum cleaner to remove grit and dirt, then the application of fuller's earth or, for some stubborn grease and oil stains, with carbon tetrachloride (inflammable). New fabrics can be washed in soft water and mild soap flakes. Textiles may be decorated by dyeing, tinting, and with specially manufactured textile colors, the latter being applied with a brush or through a stencil or screen. (See Chapter 11.)

Turpentine

A paint thinner and a cleaner for brushes used with oil colors. Children should be cautioned to handle it with care, for it is inflammable and toxic if taken internally. When using turpentine to clean brushes, press the cleaner well into the hairs, but avoiding scrubbing. Then wash brush under warm water with mild soap. A brush that is to be used again shortly can be dipped in turpentine and then tightly sealed with cellophane or Saran Wrap. It will remain pliable for a few days.

Varnish

Usually a solution of resin in alcohol or turpentine solvent. This solvent evaporates, leaving the resin film on the surface of the wood being treated. Light will eventually cause a varnish to become cloudy, then opaque, but this takes many years. Varnish is best applied with a spray gun in a dust-free room. A warm, dry day is best for varnishing. Never work in a draft, for the small dust particles in the air may drop onto the surface, causing minute specks. A large brush may also be used for application, in which case work with the wood grain, not against it. When applying varnish to oil paintings as a final sealer, the recommended type is dammar varnish, or, as second choice, mastic. Always wait at least six months before applying to a completed painting. If working in a cold room, heat the varnish slightly for best results.

Water Color

Comes in cake, tubed, or powdered form. Each has its advantages and shortcomings. The cakes are easiest to use, store indefinitely, and often cost less. Caked colors need only be lightly rubbed with a brush dipped in water. The tubed colors can be intermixed, are usually of highest quality, but do have a tendency to dry out if not tightly capped between uses. Tubed colors should be squeezed out onto a glass mixing palette like oil paints, then mixed as desired to create hues and shades, and diluted with water before application to the water-color paper. Powdered colors must be stored in a water-tight container to prevent caking. These colors are the least expensive. In addition, there is casein paint, with which you can imitate a delicate water-color wash, thick tempera, or oil paint. It is a water-base color, dries quickly, and forms a permanent, waterproof finish.

Acknowledgments

THE AUTHOR IS INDEBTED to many skilled artists, craftsmen and educators for the wide variety of unusual projects which are included in this volume. Expert advice and assistance was rendered by the editorial board of *Design* magazine and the following firms and individuals:

American Crayon Company; McCall Corporation; Art Institute of Chicago; E. I. Du Pont de Nemours; Dennison Mfg. Company; Studio of Binney and Smith, Inc.; X-Acto, Inc.; Prang Studio; Sculp-Metal Corporation; Ben Walters Company; Staley Mfg. Company; Peter Hunt; Jerry White; Michael Kosinski; Edward Winter; Thelma Winter; Victoria Bedford Betts; Betty Gage; Art Tanchon; Freda Harrington; Sam Kramer; Robert Bartlett; Julie Turner; Sister Magdalen Mary; Immaculate Heart College; Ohio State University; Manuel Barkan; Dong Kingman; Museum of Modern Art of New York; John Lynch; Howard Crist; Robert Darr Wert; Don Walker; Jules Petrancs; June Weaver; Roger Easton; Opal Hull; Sister Mary Louise; Anthony T. Polley; Des Moines *Register & Tribune*.